Fondue, Flambé
and
Side Table Cooking

BEE NILSON

Fondue, Flambé
and
Side Table Cooking

Cookery Book Club

This edition published by
The Cookery Book Club
St Giles House, 49/50 Poland Street
London WIA 2LG
by arrangement with Pelham Books Ltd

Printed in Great Britain by
Redwood Press Limited
Trowbridge, Wiltshire
and bound by the Dorstel Press, Harlow

Contents

Illustrations

1 Introduction

Fondue, flambé and side table cooking are all processes requiring equipment other than the oven and hob of a conventional cooker. This book, therefore, is not only about special methods of cooking but also about portable cooking apparatus which can be used wherever you like, in the dining room, out of doors on terrace or patio, or even camping and picnicking. Naturally some pieces of apparatus are more versatile than others.

One of the many advantages of this kind of cooking is that most of it is very quickly completed. You will find very few recipes here which take more than 45 minutes to cook, very many taking 15 minutes or less. Many of the recipes are for dishes which must have last-minute cooking and, unless the dining room is also the kitchen, the cook always has to disappear to prepare them, or, more likely, leave them out of her menus. With cooking apparatus on a side table she can stay with guests or family and they can enjoy watching, and helping. It is informal and flexible dining which suits our way of life today.

Collecting equipment for this kind of cooking could entail a considerable initial expenditure, though a surprising amount can be accomplished with a single portable hotplate, as many the owner of a bed-sitter knows. Such a hotplate can be used on the side table for flambés and other cooking, or on the dining table for fondues. Modern hotplates are thermostatically controlled and look sufficiently attractive to have on the table. The essential with either gas or electric hotplates is to see that they are connected up in such a way that there is no danger of an accident from trailing flex or faulty connections.

An alternative to the hotplate is a large spirit burner with a trivet. This has no problem of installation but needs filling with methylated spirits and can become too smelly for comfort in a small or ill-ventilated dining room.

People with kitchen/dining rooms often have the hob of a

split-level cooker installed on a table top dividing kitchen and dining area. This is ideal for side table cooking.

The electric frypans (also called skillets or automatic cookers) are more specialised pieces of apparatus. They are usually large square pans with rounded corners, a bit deeper than most frying pans, more like a sauté pan. There is an enclosed heating element underneath and the thermostatic control is usually in the handle which may be removable; if this is not the case instructions are given for how far it is safe to immerse the handle when washing the pan. If the pan has a lid this extends the possible range of cooking.

The frypan can be used for flambés, and some people recommend them for meat fondues, but I think they are too shallow for this kind of cooking. They are wonderful for all frying operations, and for sautés, as well as for jobs like poaching fish and making fruit compotes; also for girdle (griddle) cooking. These uses I have described on pages 103–123.

A description of the special portable equipment made for fondues will be found on pages 13 and 29; for flambé cooking on page 51; grilling, page 133; spit roasting, page 143.

Most well-equipped homes have a food warmer of some kind which is an invaluable aid in the service of all kinds of meals and essential for flambé and side table cooking. This may be a simple candle-heated warmer, a spirit burner warmer, an electric warming plate, or a heated trolley. On this will go plates and any hot sauces or vegetables to be served with the main dish.

If the meal is likely to be delayed for some time, the choice of these accompaniments is important. For example, rice, or a pasta in a sauce, keep better than potatoes; a salad is better than a green vegetable kept hot. Vegetables which keep hot without losing too much flavour are broad beans, green peas, carrots, celery, butter beans, red cabbage, hot beetroot in a sauce, creamed corn, or onions in a sauce,

With many of the recipes I have made suggestions for possible accompaniments, recipes for which will be found at the end of the book under Sauces, and Salads and Other Accompaniments.

NOTE: When frying temperatures are given in recipes these are for thermostat settings on an electric frypan.

° = °Fahrenheit   °C. = °Centigrade

2 Weights and Measures

ALL MEASURES USED IN THIS BOOK ARE LEVEL MEASURES

Both weights and measures are given in the recipes because some prefer to weigh when cooking and others like measuring. Either method gives good results provided reasonable care is taken.

MEASURES

1 cup (c.)	$= \frac{1}{2}$ an Imperial pint or 10 fluid ounces. = 284 millilitres (when using millilitre measures count it a scant 300 millilitres).
1 tablespoon (Tbs.)	= 15 millilitres or the size of a medicinal tablespoon.
1 teaspoon (tsp.)	= 5 millilitres or the size of a medicinal teaspoon

Imperial Weights and Measures

16 ounces (oz.)	= 1 pound (lb.)
20 fluid ounces (fl. oz.)	= 1 pint (pt.)
2 pints	= 1 quart (qt.)
8 pints	= 1 gallon

AMERICAN MEASURES

1 American cup	= 8 fluid ounces or approximately 230 millilitres (British 284 ml.)
1 American tablespoon	$= \frac{1}{2}$ fluid ounce or approximately 14 millilitres (British 15 ml.)
1 American teaspoon	$= \frac{1}{8}$ fluid ounce or approximately 5 millilitres (British 5 ml.)
1 American pint	= 16 fluid ounces (British 20 fl. oz.)

If standard American cups and spoons are used with this book, the spoons can be taken as being the same size as those used in the recipes, but count 1 cup as equivalent to 1¼ American cups.

METRIC WEIGHTS AND MEASURES

In all recipes British weights and many of the measures have been converted to the metric system. This has not been done with tablespoons and teaspoons because these are the same size as spoons used in many countries which use the metric system.

The conversion has been adjusted to give practical metric weights and measures which are still sufficiently accurate to give good results.

The following figures have been used.

1 ounce (oz.)	= 25–30 grammes (g.) (real value 28·35 g.)
1 pound (lb.)	= ½ kilogramme (kg.) (real value 453·6 g.)
	= 500 grammes
2 pounds	= 1 kilogramme (real value 2·2 lb.)
	= 1,000 grammes
1 pint (pt.)	= ½ litre (l.) (real value 568·2 millilitres)
	= 5 decilitres (dl.)
1 inch (in.)	= 2½ centimetres (cm.) (real value 2·54 cm.)
	= 25 millimetres (mm.)
1 fluid ounce (fl. oz.)	= 25–30 millilitres (ml.) (real value 28·4 ml.)
1 litre	= 1,000 millilitres or 10 decilitres

Other Useful Approximations

¼ pint	= 1½ decilitres or 150 millilitres
½ pint	= ¼ litre or 250 millilitres or 2½ decilitres
¼ pound	= 125 grammes
½ pound	= 250 grammes or ¼ kilogramme

3 Cheese Fondues

The word *fondue* comes from the French 'fondre', meaning to melt, and was originally applied to cheese dishes, either the cheese fondue familiar to most visitors to Switzerland or to cheese and egg mixtures which are baked in the oven.

Today the word 'fondue' is also used for a method of cooking, in a communal pot, and as well as cheese fondues we have meat and fish fondues (frying in oil), and fondue Chinoise or Chinese Hotpot (cooking in stock).

ESSENTIALS FOR A CHEESE FONDUE

The Cooking Pot
The best is a thick, heat-resistant pot, wide in relation to its depth, with a rounded inside bottom, and preferably suitable for using on an

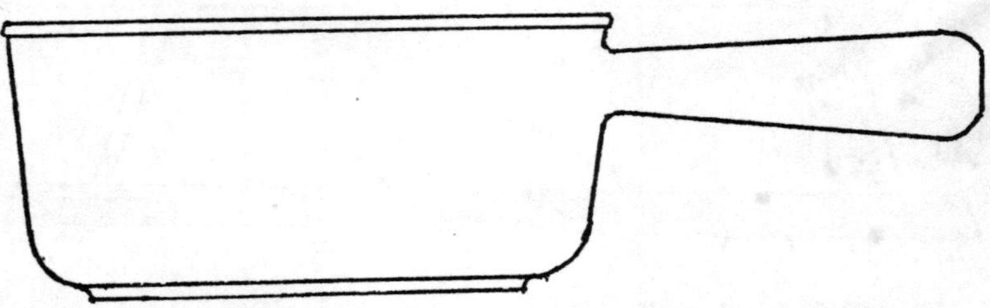

1. Cheese fondue pot, lid removed. Enamelled cast iron.

electric hotplate or gas burner. It should have a short handle like a saucepan, though this is a convenience rather than a necessity.

The metal pots sold for meat fondues are not always satisfactory for a cheese fondue, which is understandable when one realises that their requirements are rather different, the cheese fondue needing a more gentle heat and a thicker pan.

A cheese fondue pot suitable for using on a hotplate can be used for many other cooking purposes and many people already own suitable pans or casseroles. I favour one of the enamelled cast-iron pots, with a ground base for use on an electric hotplate. These are made in pretty colours and can be purchased with a lid, which makes them extra useful.

The size? I think one about 7–8 in. across the top (18–20 cm.) is about right for 4–6 people.

Heating Arrangements
The traditional Swiss cheese fondue is served over a spirit burner, but any heat source can be used, such as a camp stove, an electric

2. Methylated spirit heater for fondue pots. Black iron on wood base; spirit container white metal.

or gas hotplate or even a candle heater provided it gives enough warmth to keep the mixture bubbling gently.

When a cheese fondue is served in a restaurant the initial preparation is done in the kitchen and then the already bubbling fondue is brought to table and put on a trivet over the spirit burner. In the home there is no reason why it shouldn't all be done at table though unless you have a fairly big heater the initial cooking can be a fairly slow job. This is where a thermostatically controlled electric hotplate wins as it can be turned up high for the initial cooking and then low enough to maintain the right heat. It doesn't look as cosy or authentic as the spirit burner but there is no smell from it such as comes from some burners. The essential is to have a convenient electric point where dangerous flex is not left trailing about for people to trip over. For patio cooking the electric one has obvious advantages if a breeze is blowing.

For Serving
Provide each person with a plate, knife and fork and the special long-handled fork for spearing the bread and dipping it in the fondue. Some favour three-pronged forks as being more likely to keep the bread firmly in place. Some forks are made with prongs specially designed to grip the bread well. The idea of the knife and fork is that the bread, when coated with hot cheese, is transferred to the plate and eaten with a knife and fork. This is not only more hygienic than sticking the fondue fork in one's mouth but also allows time for the cheese to cool a little before eating; otherwise burnt tongues and lips can result. The alternative method is to hold the fondue fork with the dipped bread on it over your plate and rotate it to stop the cheese from falling off until it is cool enough to eat from the fondue fork.

Bread can be served in a basket or bowl and already cut in 1 in. (2½ cm.) cubes. Alternatively serve each person with a one-inch-thick slice of bread and let them break or cut it as they like.

If new bread is used it is advisable to have plenty of crust, as with a French loaf, or to toast the bread, but with stale bread this isn't necessary. Avoid crumbly bread such as very coarse-textured wholemeal. A close-textured wholemeal is suitable, as is rye bread, and some people use boiled potatoes instead of bread, though these should not be the floury kind; waxy or new potatoes are the best.

The proper way of using the fondue fork is to spear the piece of bread and stir it in the fondue in a figure of eight. This keeps the fondue well mixed. Each person in turn (with a maximum of 6–8 to one pot) dips a piece of bread into the fondue. At fondue parties various penalties are exacted from anyone who loses a piece of bread in the pot. A woman must kiss all the men and a man must provide a bottle of wine for the guests.

For Drinking
This is controversial. Drinking the wrong things with cheese fondue, especially if you eat a lot of it, can be a disaster and produce great discomfort. As far as alcohol is concerned, the safest course seems to be to drink the same kind of liquor as is used in making the fondue. For some this means a glass of kirsch halfway through eating the fondue, others prefer to drink the dry white wine used in making the fondue. For non-alcoholic drinks tea is usually the best, without milk or sugar, or serve black coffee.

The Ingredients
Cheese fondue being a Swiss invention, the authentic fondue should be made with Swiss cheese. No one really knows which of three French-speaking cantons—Vaud, Valais or Geneva—first made fondue. The three cheeses used are Gruyère, Emmental and Vacherin.

La Gruyère is a mountain valley in the Fribourg Canton. There is a railway station near the village of Les Gruyères where a modern exhibition hall shows a colour film, in three languages, on how Gruyère cheese is made. Les Gruyères has a castle and the usual tourist amenities. Gruyère cheese is also made in the Cantons of Vaud and Neuchâtel. Some Gruyères are made from skim milk, but the majority are from whole milk and may be mild or ripe, when they have a sharp, dry flavour. The cheese may have some holes in it but not many, and they are very small ones, quite different from Emmental.

The name Emmental comes from the beautiful valley of the Emme river in the Berne Canton, but Emmental cheese is made in most parts of Switzerland where the cows are kept in high pasture. The cheese has a lower fat content than Gruyère, a less strong flavour, and many large holes or 'eyes'.

Vacherin is a cheese made in the Jura mountain district and is used for making Fribourg Fondue.

The Swiss naturally insist that it is not a fondue unless made with one, or a mixture of these cheeses, and nothing else gives the same bouquet as a Swiss cheese plus kirsch and a local Swiss wine. Nevertheless, very tasty concoctions can be made with other cheeses, provided that they are well-flavoured ones, and these often have the advantage that they are less inclined to become stringy if the temperature is not quite right. I think it is advisable to use wine or other alcoholic beverage of the country to which the cheese belongs,

16

though the traditional kirsch and dry wine can be used with any cheese. Other spirits such as whisky, brandy, Vermouth, gin and vodka can be substituted for the kirsch. I have seen recipes substituting milk for the wine but I think that's stretching the name fondue beyond the permissible limits.

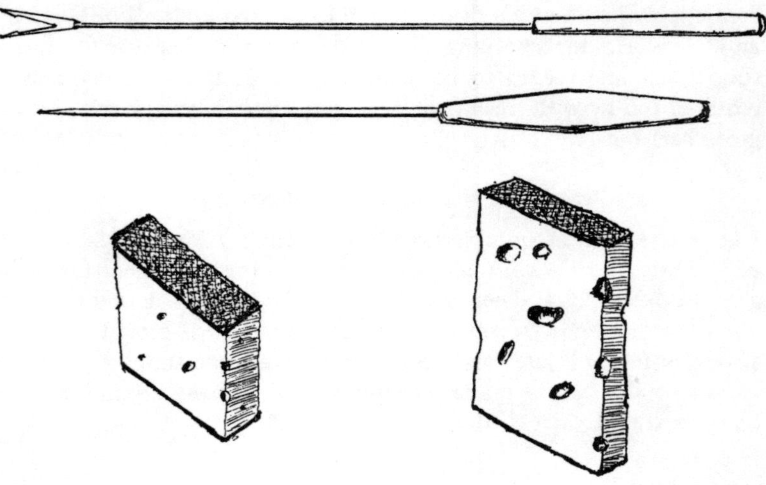

3. Fondue forks and cheeses. Top fork has fixed steel shaft and insulated handle; one below all wood, with replaceable shaft. Cheeses: left, Gruyère, right Emmental. Note different hole formation.

Some starchy binding is necessary to make a smooth mixture. Potato starch or fécule is the traditional one, but cornflour and even flour may be used. The quantity of thickening can be varied to give the desired consistency, but a fondue should not be too thick.

Cheese, kirsch, wine, potato starch, pepper, nutmeg, lemon juice and a clove of garlic to rub round the cooking pot are the ingredients of the traditional fondue but people have their own variations and if you are not bent on being traditional many other ingredients can be added such as herbs, spices and other flavourings. You can also buy ready-made Swiss fondue in a packet, and very good too.

Some fondues are made with added egg but these are usually too thick for dunking bread in and are best served in small dishes and eaten with a fork and bread or toast.

Quantities
The amount of cheese to allow per portion will vary with appetites, 4 oz. (125 g.) for a hearty appetite, down to 2 oz. (50–60 g.) for others. It isn't usually satisfactory to try to make a traditional fondue with less than a total of 8 oz. (250 g.) of cheese.

Accompaniments
Apart from bread and a drink, which I included under 'For Serving' and 'For Drinking', nothing else is usually needed because fondue is substantial and meant to be a meal in itself. If something else is required follow with fresh fruit or a fruit salad. Some people serve a green salad instead of fruit.

FONDUE FOR EMERGENCY CATERING

I keep a reserve of suitable bread in the freezer for emergencies. A bag of bread cubes will thaw very quickly at room temperature or in a warm oven. Thick slices (1 in. or 2 cm.) can be frozen and are very good toasted while frozen and then cut in cubes. If grated cheese is also kept in the freezer and you always have some suitable liquid at hand a fondue can be made very quickly. The cheese doesn't have to be thawed first.

GRUYÈRE FONDUE

The first fondue I had in the valley of La Gruyère was a disappointment, not in its texture which was marvellously smooth and creamy, but in the fact that the chef had been rather heavy-handed with the garlic, which drowned the subtle flavour of the cheese. So beware, even the experts can make mistakes.

The Swiss generally use a mixture of two or more Gruyère cheeses and thus the flavour of the final result can vary from place to place. The blend is most likely to be with a mature, full-flavoured cheese and a milder one, but Swiss fondue can be made successfully with the quality of Gruyère which is exported.

Quantities for 4–6.

A cut clove of garlic

Rub the cheese fondue pot with this.

1 *lb. Gruyère cheese* ($\frac{1}{2}$ *kg.*)

Grate coarsely and put in a bowl.

18

2–3 *tsp. potato flour*   3 *fluid oz. kirsch (6 Tbs.)*

Put the flour in a small basin and mix smooth with the kirsch.

½ *pt. dry white wine (1 c. or 250 ml.)*
1 *Tbs. lemon juice (optional)*

Put this in the fondue pot and heat to boiling. Remove from the heat. Add the cheese and stir with a wooden spoon, over a moderate heat until the mixture is smooth and boiling. Add the kirsch mixture and stir until it boils again.

Pepper   *Grated nutmeg*

Season to taste and keep bubbling very gently all the time. If it cools down it tends to go stringy. Stirring in a figure of eight as each piece of bread is dipped in helps to keep it smooth.

EMMENTAL FONDUE

This is a mild-flavoured fondue, but inclined to become stringy unless well stirred when each piece of bread is dipped into it. It can be made with the various imitation Emmental cheeses, and the American 'Swiss' cheese.

Quantities for 4–6.

A cut clove of garlic

Rub the cheese fondue pot with this.

1 *lb. Emmental cheese (½ kg.)*

Grate coarsely and put in a bowl.

2–3 *tsp. potato flour*   3 *fluid oz. kirsch (6 Tbs.)*

Put the flour in a small basin and mix smooth with the kirsch.

½ *pt. dry white wine (1 c. or 250 ml.)*   1 *Tbs. lemon juice*

Put this in the fondue pot and heat to boiling. Remove from the heat. Add the cheese and stir with a wooden spoon, over a moderate heat until the mixture is smooth and boiling. Add the kirsch mixture and stir until it boils again

Pepper   *Grated nutmeg*

Season to taste and keep bubbling very gently all the time. If it cools down it tends to go stringy. Stirring in a figure of eight as each piece of bread is dipped in helps to keep it smooth.

NEUCHÂTEL FONDUE (also known as HALF AND HALF)

This should be made with half Gruyère cheese and half Emmental cheese. The wine should be a dry white Neuchâtel but any dry white wine can be substituted. Non-Swiss Emmental cheese or 'Swiss' cheese (U.S.A.) can be substituted for the genuine Swiss Emmental.

Quantities for 4–6.

A cut clove of garlic

Rub the cheese fondue pot with this.

8 *oz. Gruyère cheese* (250 g.)   8 *oz. Emmental cheese* (250 g.)

Grate these fairly coarsely and put in a bowl.

2–3 *tsp. potato flour*   3 *fluid oz. kirsch* (6 *Tbs.*)

Put the flour in a small basin and mix smooth with the kirsch.

½ *pt. dry white wine* (1 *c. or* 250 *ml.*)
1 *Tbs. lemon juice* (*optional*)

Put this in the fondue pot and heat to boiling. Remove from the heat and add the cheeses. Stir with a wooden spoon over a moderate heat until smooth and boiling. Add the kirsch mixture and stir until the fondue boils again.

Pepper   Grated nutmeg

Season to taste and keep bubbling very gently all the time. If it cools down it tends to go stringy. Stirring in a figure of eight as each piece of bread is dipped in helps to keep it smooth.

CAERPHILLY FONDUE

Quantities for 4.

12 *oz. grated Caerphilly cheese* (375 g.)   1 *Tbs. potato flour*

Mix these together.

1 *oz. butter* (25 g.)

Melt in a cheese fondue pot.

½ *pt. cider or beer* (1 *c. or* 250 *ml.*)
1 *tsp. Worcester sauce   Salt and pepper*

Add to the pan with the cheese and heat gently, stirring well until the cheese is melted and the mixture smooth. Serve bubbling gently. Wholemeal bread is very good with this fondue.

CANADIAN FONDUE

I don't know whether they make this in Canada but I've made it in England with imported Canadian Cheddar and Canadian whisky and it is very good, with a pleasant sharp flavour. I find it is inclined to be a bit thinner than fondues made with other cheeses but this can easily be rectified by adding some more potato flour.

Quantities for 4–6.

1 lb. strong Canadian Cheddar (½ kg.)

Grate the cheese coarsely or cut it into small dice. Put in a bowl.

1 Tbs. potato flour
3 fluid ounces of Canadian whisky (6 Tbs.)

Put the flour in a small bowl and mix smooth with the whisky.

½ pt. dry white wine (1 c. or 250 ml.)

Heat this in the fondue pot until it is just boiling. Remove from the heat and add the cheese. Return to the heat and stir with a wooden spoon until it is smooth and bubbling. Add the potato flour and whisky and bring back to the boil, stirring all the time.

Pepper   Grated nutmeg

Season to taste and serve bubbling, as with other fondues. Should it still be too thin, add a little more potato flour blended with cold water.

CHEDDAR FONDUE WITH BEER

Quantities for 4–6.

1 clove of cut garlic

Rub the fondue pot with this.

½ pt. beer (1 c. or 250 ml.)

Put in the pot and heat to boiling.

12 oz. grated strong English Cheddar (375 g.)   1 Tbs. flour

Mix the cheese with the flour and add gradually to the beer, stirring until smooth.

1 tsp. Worcester sauce

Add and bring to the boil. Transfer to the fondue burner and serve in the usual way.

CHEDDAR FONDUE WITH CIDER

Quantities for 4.

> 2–3 *tsp. potato flour*   1 *tsp. dry mustard*   *Pepper*
> ½ *pt. dry cider* (1 *c. or* 250 *ml.*)

Blend the dry ingredients to a smooth cream with a little of the cider, set aside.

> 1 *oz. butter* (25 *g.*)
> 1 *lb. strong grated Cheddar cheese* (½ *kg.*)

Melt the butter in the fondue pot, add the cheese and the remaining cider. Heat gently and stir until smooth. Add the flour mixture, turn up the heat a little and stir until it thickens. Keep bubbling gently during service. This one is very good with toast cubes instead of bread.

COTTAGE CHEESE AND EMMENTAL FONDUE

This mixture of two cheeses gives a good texture to the fondue and prevents the Emmental from becoming stringy when heated. As cottage cheese has little flavour of its own added flavourings are indicated, but these can be varied according to personal taste.

Quantities for 4.

> 8 *oz. cottage cheese* (250 *g.*)   8 *oz. Emmental* (250 *g.*)

If you want a very smooth fondue rub the cottage cheese through a sieve, otherwise, mash it before adding it to the coarsely grated Emmental.

> 2 *Tbs. potato flour*   ½ *tsp. dry mustard*
> ½ *tsp. paprika pepper*   ½ *tsp. anchovy essence*
> 1–2 *tsp. Worcester sauce*   4 *Tbs. cream*

Mix these together until smooth.

> ½ *pt. dry cider* (1 *c. or* 250 *ml.*)

Heat to almost boiling in the fondue pot, add the cheese and stir and cook until it melts and the mixture bubbles. Add the blended starch mixture and stir until it thickens.

> 2 *Tbs. chopped chives or other green herbs*

Add, mix in and serve bubbling in the usual way.

CRAB FONDUE

Quantities for 4.

8 oz. Caerphilly cheese, coarsely grated (250 g.)
5 Tbs. dry white wine   1 tsp. lemon juice   Pepper
3–4 oz. canned, fresh or frozen crab meat (75–125 g.)

Drain and flake the crab meat removing any bony bits. Frozen crab may be used frozen or partially thawed. Heat all the ingredients together, stirring well until the cheese melts.

Serve in the usual way. When it becomes too thick for this turn it out onto plates and finish eating with a fork.

ENGLISH SAGE CHEESE FONDUE

This can be made with mature Sage Derby cheese or with English Cheddar cheese and fresh chopped sage leaves, which is very good indeed. You might think the sage would be too strong for the cheese but the blend of flavours here is very pleasant.

Quantities for 4–6

½ pt. dry cider (1 c. or 250 ml.)

Put in the fondue pot and bring to the boil. Remove from the heat and add

1 lb. mature English Cheddar cheese (½ kg.), coarsely grated

Return to a moderate heat and stir gently until the cheese is melted and the mixture bubbling.

2–3 tsp. potato flour   1 Tbs. lemon juice

Blend these together and stir into the fondue, stirring until it thickens.

Pepper to taste   2 Tbs. fresh, finely-chopped sage, or to taste

Add and serve the fondue with the usual squares of stale bread. I use bread toasted on one side of the thick slices and then cut in pieces.

ENGLISH-SWISS HALF AND HALF FONDUE

This one is very good indeed, smoother in texture than the traditional Half and Half or Neuchâtel fondue, page 20.

Quantities for 4–6.

A cut clove of garlic

Rub the cheese fondue pot with this.

8 *oz. strong English Cheddar* (250 g.)   8 *oz. Gruyère* (250 g.)

Grate these fairly coarsely and put in a bowl.

2–3 *tsp. potato flour*   3 *fluid oz. kirsch* (6 *Tbs.*)

Put the flour in a small basin and mix smooth with the kirsch.

½ *pt. dry white wine* (1 *c. or* 250 *ml.*)   1 *Tbs. lemon juice*

Put this in the fondue pot and heat to boiling. Remove from the heat and add the cheeses. Stir with a wooden spoon over a moderate heat until smooth and boiling. Add the kirsch mixture and stir until the fondue boils again.

Pepper   Grated nutmeg

Season to taste and keep bubbling very gently all the time. Put over the table heater and serve in the usual way.

FONDUE WITH CIDER AND GIN

This is a good combination for a fondue, dry cider and Dutch or English gin. There is a slight difference of flavour with each gin but this is not as pronounced as when the two are served as drinks.

I have made the fondue with Dutch Gouda cheese and the flavour was very good but I find the cheese difficult to melt down completely. However, one doesn't notice this lack of smoothness when eating it in the normal fondue manner. It is apparent if, as we do, you tip the last of the fondue onto a plate and eat it with a spoon. If you want a completely smooth fondue I suggest substituting Cheddar or Cheshire cheese for the Gouda.

Quantities for 4–6.

1 *lb. Gouda, Cheddar or Cheshire cheese* (½ *kg.*)

Grate the cheese coarsely and put it in a dish.

1 *Tbs. potato flour*   6 *Tbs. gin*

Mix to a smooth cream.

½ *pt. dry cider*   (1 *c. or* 250 *ml.*)

Put in the fondue pot and bring to the boil. Remove from the heat and add the cheese, stirring until it melts. Then heat to boiling and add the gin mixture, stir until it thickens.

Pepper   Grated nutmeg

Season to taste. I like plenty of nutmeg with this one. Serve in the usual way, bubbling over the spirit burner.

24

FONDUE PROVENÇALE

Quantities for 4.

> *About ¼ clove crushed garlic or to taste*
> *½ pt. dry white wine (1 c. or 250 ml.)*

Put in the cheese fondue pot and heat to boiling.

> *8 oz. grated Gruyère cheese (250 g.)*
> *8 oz. grated Emmental cheese (250 g.)*

Remove the wine from the heat and add the cheese. Stir and cook over a moderate heat until the cheese is completely melted.

> *2–3 tsp. potato flour   3 oz. (6 Tbs.) dry French vermouth*

Mix the potato flour smooth with the vermouth and stir into the fondue, stirring and heating until it thickens.

> *2 Tbs. chopped green herbs which can include parsley, chives, tarragon and marjoram; or just parsley and tarragon, or parsley and marjoram.*

Add to the fondue and mix in. Serve the fondue, bubbling in the usual way, with cubes of crusty bread.

FONDUE WITH WALNUTS AND BRANDY

Quantities for 4–6.

> *1 lb. strong Cheddar or Cheshire cheese (½ kg.)*
> *2 oz. ground walnuts (50 g.)*

Grate the cheese coarsely and put it in a bowl. Grind the walnuts finely, either in an electric blender or a mincer. Add to the cheese.

> *2–3 tsp. potato flour   2 Tbs. brandy*

Blend until smooth and set aside. If you like your fondue to be fairly thick use the larger amount of flour.

> *½ pt. dry cider or white wine (1 c. or 250 ml.)*

Heat this in the fondue pot until it is almost boiling. Add the cheese and walnuts and stir until the cheese has melted and the mixture is boiling. Add the blended potato flour and stir until the fondue thickens and boils again. Serve bubbling in the usual way with cubes of bread or toast.

SOFT CHEESE FONDUE

This has a milder cheese flavour than most other fondues but the combination of ketchup, onion and other flavourings makes it interesting. Use full-fat cream cheese or other soft cheese. If you use a low-fat cottage cheese you will need to add double cream in place of the milk in the recipe.

Quantities for 3–4.

2 *eggs*   8 *oz. cream cheese or other soft cheese* (250 g.)

Beat the eggs in the fondue pot, add the cheese and mix it thoroughly with the eggs using a wooden spoon to break it up.

2 *Tbs. tomato ketchup*   4 *Tbs. milk or cream*
¼ *tsp. paprika pepper or to taste*
2 *Tbs. finely-chopped onion*
2 *Tbs. white wine or cider*

Add to the egg and cheese mixture, combine well and heat to boiling, stirring gently all the time. Simmer until it thickens; if too thick, add some more wine or cider. Serve with bread in the usual way.

SOUR CREAM FONDUE

A non-alcoholic fondue with a smooth texture and a very pleasant mild flavour.

Quantities for 4.

8 *oz. strong Cheddar cheese* (250 g.)   1 *tsp. potato flour*

Grate the cheese coarsely and put it in the fondue pot. Sprinkle the potato flour over it and mix.

½ *pt. sour or cultured cream* (1 c. or 250 ml.)
1 *tsp. Worcester sauce*   2 *tsp. very finely chopped onion*

Add to the cheese, mix and heat, stirring all the time until the cheese has melted and the mixture is bubbling. Serve with bread or toast in the usual way.

SWISS-ENGLISH FONDUE WITH BEER

Quantities for 4.

1 *clove garlic*

Rub the fondue pot with the cut clove of garlic.

½ pt. beer (1 c. or 250 ml.)

Put in the pot and heat to boiling.

8 oz. grated Gruyère or Emmental cheese (250 g.)
4 oz. grated strong Cheddar cheese (125 g.)   1 Tbs. flour

Mix the cheese with the flour and add to the beer, gradually, stirring until smooth.

1 tsp. Worcester sauce

Add and bring to the boil. Transfer to the fondue burner. Serve in the usual way.

TOMATO AND CHEESE FONDUE

Quantities for 3–4.

½ Tbs. butter   4 Tbs. sour cream
½–1 small rasher streaky bacon finely chopped
2 thin slices onion finely chopped
8 oz. coarsely grated cheese (250 g.), Cheddar, Gouda or Emmental
2 Tbs. tomato paste   ½ tsp. potato flour   Pepper
Fresh chopped marjoram or tarragon or use some dried herbs
About ½ pt. white wine (1 c. or 250 ml.)

Put all together in the fondue pot, adding about three-quarters of the wine to begin with and the rest if it is needed at the end. Stir over a moderate heat until the cheese is melted and the mixture bubbling. Serve bubbling, with cubes of bread or toast in the usual way.

CHEESE FONDUE WITH EGG

Quantities for 3–4.

4 oz. strong Cheddar or Caerphilly cheese (125 g.)

Cut the cheese in small pieces, or grate it. Put in a cheese fondue pot.

1 tsp. dry mustard   Pinch cayenne pepper
4 Tbs. cream or 2 Tbs. cream and 2 Tbs. sherry

Mix mustard and pepper to a smooth cream with the liquid, add to the cheese.

1 egg

Beat well and add to the cheese. Cook over a gentle heat until the cheese is melted and the mixture thickens. Keep just warm during service. If it seems too thick for a fondue, thin with cream.

The two recipes which follow are technically fondues but are too thick to serve in the fondue pot, although they are cooked in the pot. They are served in small hot dishes with toast or dry biscuits handed separately.

THICK CHEESE FONDUE (no alcohol)

Quantities for 4.

2 oz. butter (50 g.)

Melt in the fondue pot.

4 eggs   4 oz. grated Gruyère cheese (125 g.)
Salt and pepper   Pinch of mace

Beat the eggs thoroughly and add all ingredients to the melted butter. Cook over a fairly quick heat, stirring all the time until the mixture thickens. Pour into small hot dishes and serve with a table fork and toast or bread.

THICK CHEESE FONDUE WITH EGG AND SHERRY

Quantities for 6.

1 oz. butter (25 g.)

Melt in the fondue pot.

6 eggs, beaten   8 oz. grated strong Cheddar cheese (250 g.)
Salt and pepper   6 Tbs. dry or medium sherry

Add to the melted butter and cook over a moderate heat, stirring all the time until the mixture is smooth and thick. Serve in small hot dishes, to be eaten with a fork, or serve on toast.

4 Meat and Fish Fondues

The Cooking Pot

This needs to be made of a material that will withstand the high temperatures needed for frying and which will transmit heat quickly so that the cooking oil maintains a reasonable temperature even though cold food is constantly being added to it. Metal is usually the most satisfactory material, either copper or stainless steel, though iron pots are favoured by some. The cast-iron pot has an advantage in being heavy, retaining heat well, and being more stable and less likely to be knocked over (one of the hazards of having a pot of hot oil on the dining table), but it is slower to heat up.

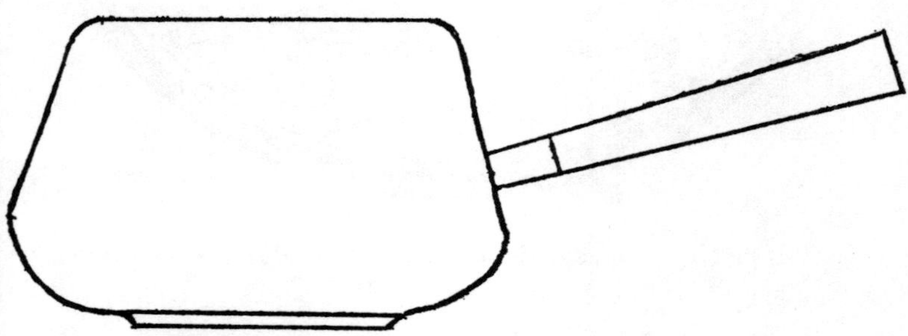

4. Fondue Bourguignonne pot, lid removed. Stainless steel.

Most of the pots specially made for fondues are wider at the base than the top and are deeper than a cheese fondue pot. The best have a guard to minimise the splashing of fat during cooking.

Alternatives to these special pots are any deep metal pans of a suitable shape and size for deep fat frying. Others are the modern thermostatically controlled deep fat fryers (useful in the kitchen too for chips and other foods); or an electric frypan or skillet which is

5. Heat preserver and splash protector for Fondue Bourguignonne pot, white metal.

also thermostatically controlled, though these are rather wide and shallow to be ideal for the job and fat splashing can be a problem.

Heating Arrangements
The automatic deep fat fryer and the electric frypan have their own built-in heating elements and the fact that they are thermostatically controlled is an advantage when it comes to judging the right temperature of the oil.

The special metal fondue pots are placed on a trivet over a spirit

30

burner, the oil having first been heated to frying temperature on the kitchen hotplate. Other types of cooking pots can be used on a thermostatically controlled electric hotplate placed on the table, provided precautions are taken to see that it is impossible for a trailing flex to be the cause of a spill and burning disaster.

Because the cooking medium is hot oil, usually in a pot over a naked flame, there is always an element of danger from spills and burns and a risk of fire. I think it is unwise to let children use this kind of meat fondue apparatus unless they are very closely supervised, and that it is a very risky thing to have it at a buffet party as some people recommend. If you do use it under these conditions make sure that a fire extinguisher is at hand and a first-aid kit for treating burns. This may sound alarmist, but we all know what a lot of terrible accidents do happen in the home.

My own view is that the meat fondue is best for an adult party, preferably not more than four people to one pot, so that all can easily reach the pot and thus reduce the danger of knocking it over. I noticed, in a well-known fondue restaurant in Lausanne, that small pans were used, one for each pair of guests, and I think this is better than having a large one, though, of course, rather expensive in initial outlay for home use. I also approved the fact that this restaurant only served fondues in one dining room, in the basement, so that non-fondue eaters would not be annoyed by the smell of cooking oil. Those eating the fondue don't usually notice the smell, but others do.

Choosing and Preparing the Meat
Allow about 4–5 oz. per person (125–150 g.). While Fondue Bourguignonne is traditionally made with beef, any meat suitable for frying can be used for a fondue, including a mixture of meats.

The important point is that the cuts used should be tender ones, only those suitable for grilling or frying. Frozen meat can be used but it must be completely defrosted (and at room temperature to avoid over-cooling the oil). All meats should be well dried (to avoid making the oil splutter). Dry on paper kitchen towels.

Beef is usually cut in small cubes, about ½–¾ in. (1–1½ cm.) and this is also a suitable size for other meats if you like them slightly pink in the middle. Meats such as pork, which should be well cooked, are best cut in strips, about ¼ in. thick (½ cm.); but make sure they are a suitable size for easy handling with the fondue forks. I prefer to have veal cut in strips too.

Keep all meat refrigerated until about an hour before the meal, then allow it to come to room temperature. Remove all fat and cut the meat in pieces either just before serving or when it comes out of the refrigerator.

The Oil
Use enough oil to fill the pot $\frac{1}{3}$–$\frac{1}{2}$ full. The best is peanut or ground nut oil because it is practically tasteless and odourless.

After use, allow the oil to cool in the fondue pot, then strain through muslin or a very fine sieve. Return to the bottle or tin. You will probably be surprised to see how little of the oil has in fact been used up. The number of times one lot of oil can be used will vary with the amount and kind of food being cooked and the temperature used. Over-heating causes rapid deterioration in its quality. A dark colour and unpleasant smell indicate spoilage.

Unless you are using an automatic electric fryer you will need a thermometer to tell when the oil is hot. It should register 375–400° (190–200°C) to be hot enough for the fondue.

Serving
Special plates are sold for serving meat fondue, usually ceramic, with shallow compartments, small ones for the sauces and a larger one for the meat. While these are colourful and convenient for washing up they are not essential. Separate tiny dishes or saucers (coffee cup size) can be used for the sauces and look very attractive. Arrange the meat on a small plate, one for each guest, and put the sauce dishes in a semi-circle round the plate. The alternative is to put a plate of meat between each pair of guests. Garnish the meat with parsley or other greenery.

In addition, provide an ordinary table knife and fork and a long-handled fondue fork. An alternative to the fondue fork is a long, pointed wooden stick in a holder. These are sold in sets with the holders and the pointed stick is meant to be thrown away after use.

The way to cook meat fondue is for each guest to spear a piece of meat and put it in the cooking pot. When the meat is browned or cooked to taste it is transferred to the table fork while the next piece of meat goes into the pot. The cooked piece is dipped in a sauce and eaten. The fondue fork gets very hot in the fat and it is dangerous to try and eat the meat from it.

For Drinking
Wine is the usual drink served with meat fondues, the choice depending on personal taste and the kind of meat being cooked. You can stick to red wines with red meats and white wine with white meats, or just please yourself. If you are eating the fondue in a restaurant the waiter will naturally try and sell you the idea that only wine is appropriate to a meat fondue but you don't have to follow his advice and beer or anything else can be taken instead.

Accompaniments
The basics are some sauces and some bread. Other items can be added according to taste. Below is a list of suggestions and in the individual recipes I have given my personal selection.

The sauces most commonly served with fondues in restaurants are made with a mayonnaise base with different flavourings added, such as horseradish, curry, garlic and so on. I think these are a mistake for a number of reasons. Although the meat soaks up very little oil during cooking it still has an oily outside, and to dip it in an oil sauce such as mayonnaise seems too much of the same thing. If you want to serve a fatty sauce I think butter, cream (fresh or soured), or egg yolk are better ingredients. Furthermore I think all mayonnaise-based sauces taste similar despite small amounts of different flavourings, and I am not impressed by a restaurant which advertises that it serves 'five luscious sauces' with its Fondue Bourguignonne and all five are in fact mayonnaise. In addition there is the question of boring monotony in texture.

The one essential as far as I am concerned is that the sauce should have a good flavour which goes with the flavour of the meat. Give a choice of three or four different ones, or more, according to taste.

It is often difficult to gauge the amount of sauce to serve each person but you can start with something like a tablespoon of each and keep a reserve for topping up if one proves a favourite. In the interests of hygiene any sauce left in the guests' dishes should, of course, be thrown away.

Most of the sauces can be made in advance and stored in the refrigerator or freezer and many can be purchased ready-made.

MEAT FONDUE ACCOMPANIMENTS

Instead of Bread
Potatoes—crisps, straw, baked jacket or boiled.

Rice—plain boiled or rice with herbs, page 190 or saffron rice, page 192.

Sauces
Anchovy butter, page 170
Béarnaise, page 172
Breton, page 173
Chilli sauce, bottled
Cranberry, canned or page 174
Cumberland, page 174
Curry butter, page 170
Curry mayonnaise, page 169
Curry sauce, canned, or page 174
Fennel mayonnaise, page 169
Garlic butter, page 171
Garlic mayonnaise, page 169
Herb sauce, page 176
Horseradish, bottled, or page 177
Ketchup and cream, page 177
Lemon sauce, page 177
Maître d'hôtel butter, page 171
Mayonnaise, page 168
Mayonnaise Aurore, page 169
Mint butter, page 171
Mint sauce, page 178
Mushroom ketchup, bottled
Mustard, bottled, or page 178
Mustard butter, page 171
Paprika butter, page 171
Paprika mayonnaise, page 169
Remoulade sauce, page 170
Salsa verde, page 179
Savoury butters, page 170
Sour cream sauce, page 180
Soy sauce, bottled
Soy sauce with ginger, page 180
Sweet chutney sauce, page 173
Tarragon butter, page 172
Tartare sauce, page 170
Tomato ketchup, bottled

Tomato sauce, page 180
Vinaigrette, page 181
Worcestershire, bottled

Other Accompaniments
Beetroot, pickled
Chives, chopped
Chutney
Cucumber, pickled or chopped fresh
Herbs, fresh chopped
Lemon wedges, especially with veal, pork and liver
Nuts
Olives, plain or stuffed
Onions, small pickled or fresh spring
Parsley, chopped
Peppers, sliced raw sweet red or green
Pickles, any kind
Salt, seasoned (garlic, onion, celery)
Tomato, raw sliced or diced
Watercress, sprigs or chopped

For those who like Sweet Things
Fruit, canned, drained
Fruit, preserved in brandy
Fruit, sweet pickled
Ginger in syrup

Salads
Carrot and apple, page 184
Grapefruit and beetroot, page 185
Mixed green, page 185
Mushroom, page 186
Orange, page 186
Orange and onion, page 187
Tomato and sweet pepper, page 187

FONDUE BOURGUIGNONNE

Quantities for 4.

$1-1\frac{1}{2}$ *lb. lean beef steak* ($\frac{1}{2}-\frac{3}{4}$ *kg.*)

Use either fillet, rump, or sirloin steak, well hung. Trim off any fat
(allow for this when buying the steak). Cut the meat in $\frac{1}{2}-\frac{3}{4}$ in. (1–2

cm.) cubes and arrange on small plates or in a fondue plate. Garnish with any greenery available or with pickles.

Peanut or ground nut oil 1–1½ pt. (½–¾ l.)

Put oil in the fondue pot to make it just less than half full. Heat to 375° (190°C). Transfer the pot to the fondue burner. Provide fondue forks for spearing the meat for cooking and a knife and fork for eating the meat.

Accompaniments
Any listed on pages 33–35.
Specially recommended: Worcester sauce or soy sauce; horseradish sauce, page 177; mustard sauce, page 178; Béarnaise sauce, page 172; garlic butter, page 171; fresh French bread or crisp rolls; mixed green salad, page 185; tomato and sweet pepper salad, page 187.

CHICKEN FONDUE

Quantities for 4.

4 chicken breasts

These can be fresh or frozen breasts. If frozen chicken is used, thaw completely and allow to come to room temperature before serving. Dry the pieces thoroughly on paper towels. Cut fresh or frozen breasts in small pieces, ½–¾ in. thick (1–2 cm.). Arrange on small plates or on a fondue plate and garnish with parsley or chervil or other material available.

Peanut or ground nut oil 1–1½ pt. (½–¾ l.)

Put oil in the fondue pot to make it just less than half full. Heat to 375° (190°C). Transfer the pot to the fondue burner. Provide fondue forks for spearing the meat for cooking and a knife and fork for eating the cooked meat. Guests cook it according to taste but it is advisable to cook chicken thoroughly, about 2 mins.

Accompaniments
Any listed on pages 33–35.
Specially recommended: Béarnaise sauce, page 172; cold curry sauce, page 174; garlic mayonnaise, page 169; cold tomato sauce, page 180; Breton sauce, page 172; fresh French bread or crisp rolls; saffron rice, page 192; mushroom salad, page 186; brussels sprouts and orange salad, page 183; chicory and olive salad, page 184.

36

FISH FONDUE

The equipment and method are essentially the same as for meat fondues but the choice of accompaniments is usually different, see below. The fish can be dipped in batter before frying. This can be rather smelly and make the dining room smell like a fish and chip shop, but is fine for out of doors.

Quantities for 4.

1½ *lb. fillets of fresh fish or shelled lobster, prawns,*
shrimps or scampi (¾ kg.)

The fish fillets should be firm or the fish will fall to pieces during frying. White or oily fish is suitable and the flat fish like turbot, halibut, sole and plaice are usually firm enough. Frozen fish is inclined to be too flabby for this and if you use it frozen or partially thawed it cools the fat too much and slows up the cooking. But keep fresh fish refrigerated until just before using it as this helps to keep it firm. Make sure it is well-dried (use paper towels), and cut it in small pieces. Arrange pieces on lettuce leaves or other greenery on individual plates or fondue dishes.

Peanut or ground nut oil 1–1½ *pt.* (½–¾ *l.*)

Put oil in the fondue pot to make it just less than half full. Heat to 375° (190°C). Transfer the pot to the fondue burner.

A piece of fish is speared with the fondue fork and cooked until it is lightly browned. Transfer to a plate to eat with a table fork.

Accompaniments
Any from the list on pages 33–35.
Specially recommended: delicious with just lemon wedges, salt (a flavoured one if you like), perhaps soy sauce too, and a mixed green salad, page 185, or cucumber or tomato salad, or tomato and sweet pepper salad, page 187.

LAMB FONDUE

Quantities for 4.

1–1½ *lb. lean meat without bone* (½–¾ *kg.*)

Use slices from the top of the leg (fillet), the 'eye' of cutlets or loin chops, or the best pieces from a boned shoulder. Trim off all fat and cut the meat in ½–¾ in. cubes (1–2 cm.). Arrange on small dishes or on a fondue plate, garnished with fresh herbs.

Peanut or ground nut oil 1–1½ pt. (½–¾ l.)

Put oil in the fondue pot to just less than half full. Heat to 375° (190°C) and transfer to the fondue burner. Provide fondue forks for spearing and cooking the meat and a table knife and fork for eating it with. Lamb is best cooked until just pink in the middle, about 1½–2 mins.

Accompaniments
Any listed on pages 33–35.
Specially recommended; curry sauce, page 174; lemon wedges or lemon sauce, page 177; Cumberland sauce, page 174; mint sauce, page 178; garlic butter, page 171; herb or saffron rice, page 192; sliced tomato and cucumber; olives; carrot and apple salad, page 184.

MINCED LAMB BALLS

Quantities for 4–6.

*1 lb. lean raw minced lamb (½ kg.)   1 large mashed potato or
1 portion mashed potato powder made up   1 tsp. curry powder
Pinch dried garlic or some fresh garlic juice to taste
2 oz. strong cheese, grated (50 g.)   ½ tsp. salt*

Mix all together thoroughly and roll into small balls about ½–¾ in. diameter (1–2 cm.)

Peanut or ground nut oil 1–1½ pt. (½–¾ l.)

Fill the fondue pot to just less than half and heat the oil to 375° (190°C). Transfer the pot to the fondue burner. If possible use the long wooden sticks to spear the balls as they may be inclined to break unless handled very carefully with the fondue forks. Fry until brown, transfer to a table fork to eat.

Accompaniments
Boiled rice with a little melted butter and plenty of chopped fresh thyme; mixed salad, page 185 ; chutney sauce, page 173; lemon wedges; sliced tomato.

MIXED MEAT FONDUE

Quantities for 4.

1–1½ lb. mixed lean meat (½–¾ kg.)

This may be a combination of any meats you like, including cubes of

38

liver and kidney. For choosing and preparing beef, see page 35; chicken, page 36; lamb, page 37; pork, page 39; veal, page 40; Tiny chipolata sausages can also be included. Liver and kidney need to be very fresh and firm or they will be difficult to handle with the fondue fork. It is a good plan to serve the meats on a large central dish or one dish between two so that people can choose their favourite meats. Keep a reserve supply to replenish favourites.

Peanut or ground nut oil 1–1½ *pt.* (½–¾ *l.*)

Put oil in the fondue pot to make it just less than half full. Heat to 375° (190°C). Transfer the pot to the fondue burner. Provide fondue forks or wooden sticks for spearing the meat and a knife and fork for eating it.

Accompaniments
Any listed on pages 33–35.
Specially recommended: Béarnaise sauce, page 172; soy sauce; garlic butter, page 171; mustard sauce, page 178; lemon wedges; pickles; herb sauce, page 176; chopped fresh herbs; fresh French bread; mushroom salad, page 186; sweet pepper salad, page 187.

PORK FONDUE

Quantities for 4.

1–1½ *lb. lean meat without bone* (½–¾ *kg.*)

Use pork fillet or the meat from the 'eye' of loin chops. Slice it very thinly and then cut the slices in pieces about 1 in. square (2½ cm.). Remove any fat. Arrange on small plates or a fondue plate, garnished with pickles.

Peanut or ground nut oil 1–1½ *pt.* (½–¾ *l.*)

Put oil in the fondue pot to just less than half full. Heat the oil to 375° (190°C) and then transfer the pot to the fondue burner. Provide fondue forks for spearing and cooking the meat and a knife and fork for eating it. Pork should be well-cooked but these thin slices will cook through in a minute or so.

Accompaniments
Any listed on pages 33–35.
Specially recommended: soy sauce; cranberry sauce, canned or page 174; tomato sauce, page 180; lemon wedges; onion or garlic salt; sweet pickled pears and peaches; pickled beetroot; apple sauce, page

172; sweet chutney sauce, page 173; brussels sprouts and orange salad, page 183.

VEAL FONDUE

Quantities for 4.

1–1½ *lb. veal* (½–¾ *kg.*)

Use veal escalopes or the 'eye' of cutlets or loin chops. The meat should be beaten until thin, but not thin enough to make it difficult to spear with the fondue fork. Cut it in strips about ¼–½ in. wide (½–1 cm.) and a length to be easily handled with the fondue fork. Arrange on lettuce leaves on small plates. Put the meat in a single layer as veal pieces are inclined to cling to each other and are difficult to spear.

Peanut or ground nut oil 1–1½ *pt.* (½–¾ *l.*)

Put oil in the fondue pot until almost half full. Heat to 375° (190°C) and then transfer the pot to the fondue burner. The thin strips of veal will cook in a few seconds.

Accompaniments
Any listed on pages 33–35.
Specially recommended: herb sauce, page 176 (parsley, chives, tarragon, lemon thyme); anchovy butter, page 170; lemon sauce, page 177; lemon wedges; tomato sauce, page 180; Breton sauce, page 173; rice with herbs, page 190; sweet pepper salad, page 187; orange salad, page 186.

GRILLED STEAK SERVED AS A MEAT FONDUE

I first met this in Berne, Switzerland, in a popular restaurant which specialises in interesting light meals and snacks. The steaks were small sirloins and there was special equipment for serving them. One consisted of a short iron skewer like a small kebab skewer, on which the cooked steak was impaled. The skewer was supported on iron brackets and underneath was a small trough to catch the juices. With the second kind the steak was served on a small iron grid with a shallow pan below. In addition to one or other of these the guest had a meat plate, knife and fork, and a number of little dishes containing sauces of the same kind as those served with a true meat fondue, see page 34. Other accompaniments included potato crisps, sliced bread, boiled rice and sliced raw red peppers. The steak was brought to the table with some warm spirit in a small pan. This was ignited and poured over the steak so it really was a combined grill, flambé and fondue. The steak was transferred to one's plate and cut in small pieces which were then dipped in the chosen sauce. This was very good to eat and in some ways more pleasant than the true meat fondue.

I've done it at home with ordinary grilled steak and the fondue sauces but no special serving apparatus and it was very satisfactory. If you want to flambé the steaks, put them on a hot heat-resistant serving dish, ignite some warm brandy or other spirit and pour it over the steaks. Then serve.

For how to grill beefsteak, see pages 133–5.

5 Chinese Hotpot

FONDUE CHINOISE OR CHINESE HOTPOT

I first ate Chinese Hotpot in Hong Kong with some Chinese friends. It was quite an experience. Six of us sat round a circular table and started our meal with small dishes containing strips of various cooked meats, asparagus, and sea plant. To follow were fresh-water shrimps with plain boiled rice and fresh green peas, all very delicate and delicious. Then came the Hotpot. First a portable gas burner was put in the centre of the table. Then a waiter wheeled up a cylinder of gas on a special trolley and connected it up to the burner. Then came a large brass pan with a curved bottom and a lid. In the pan was boiling stock and some fish balls. In a circle round this were arranged plates containing wafer-thin small slices of raw meats (pork, liver, beef, and chicken), thinly sliced raw fresh-water fish, strips of fresh ginger, the tender tips of sweet pea plants (I was assured it was the sweet pea and not the green pea), and sliced raw lettuce. Each guest had a plate, chopsticks, a bowl of rice and a small dish of soy sauce. also a bowl for the Chinese green tea drunk throughout the meal. In addition we each had what looked like a minute wire frying basket on a long handle. Each guest put some food in the basket and lowered it into the boiling stock, left it a few minutes to cook, then transferred the food to the plate to be eaten with chopsticks; but first the food was dipped in the soy sauce, or not, according to taste. When all the meat and vegetables had been eaten plates were removed and china bowls and spoons brought to the table. The stock was ladled in and we ate this as soup. The whole thing was delicious and the combination of flavours in the soup very intriguing. Since then I have cooked many anglicised versions of the hotpot and found them very enjoyable even though they didn't have all the authentic Chinese ingredients. I have come to prefer this type of fondue to the meat one using cooking oil, for it is much more pleasant to sit round a bowl of bubbling stock than one of hot oil.

A Swiss version of Fondue Chinoise I had in a restaurant in Berne, quite recently. This turned out to be a combination of a Chinese Hotpot and a Fondue Bourguignonne. There were two of us and we each had a burner, stand, and small pot of boiling stock. This apparatus was standing on a circular tray round the edge of which were small dishes containing three mayonnaise-based sauces, some chopped parsley, soy sauce, and an egg yolk. Between us we had a basket of French bread and a platter with a generous amount of sliced beef. We each had a fondue fork and a pair of chopsticks. When we had finished the meat the waiter took away the pot and cooking apparatus to a side table and produced two Chinese bowls and porcelain spoons. Before ladling the soup into these he added what remained of the egg yolk (used for dipping the meat in before cooking), the soy sauce remains and the parsley. This all made a very delicious soup.

I didn't like the idea of individual burners and pots. It seemed pointless and was uncomfortably hot to have the burner so near one's face. It may have been done for reasons of hygiene but that problem of the communal pot could be overcome by providing a table fork for eating the bits of meat, keeping the fondue fork just for the cooking; or they could import some of the Chinese cooking baskets.

Choice of Cooking Pot and Heating Arrangements
I have used both my cheese fondue pot and meat fondue pot, and either serves well on its spirit burner, so there is no need to buy special equipment for this fondue. You could also use any cooking pot on an electric hotplate or other source of heat, which needs to be enough to keep the stock bubbling gently. It is heated initially in the kitchen and brought to table already bubbling.

Serving
I put the prepared meat and fish on flat dishes one for each kind of food, in the Chinese manner. If everyone can't reach all of them they can be passed round. Each guest is given small dishes of sauces, egg if used, chopped parsley, chives or other herbs. Each also has a fondue fork, a table fork and a soup spoon. The soup is served in English-type soup bowls, and we drink wine instead of tea with the hotpot.

Ingredients
The stock can be any kind, home-made, or a cube and water. The

44

various ingredients which are cooked in it improve the quality of whatever you start with; any kind of raw meat tender enough for quick cooking and any kind of firm fish and any kind of shellfish (raw, cooked or frozen). The vegetables, too, need to be in pieces that will cook quickly, sliced green vegetables such as coarse lettuce, Chinese cabbage, tiny cauliflower flowerets, spinach leaves. Slivers of other vegetables can be added and left in longer to flavour the stock, or eventually fished out and eaten. These could include strips of carrot, red and green peppers, celery, young green beans, finely sliced onion, sliced peeled cucumber, cubed aubergine, small or halved fresh mushrooms. If you are unable to find a shop selling fresh ginger, add a teaspoon of ground ginger to the stock before serving; enough for 8 or more portions of soup.

An egg yolk can be served for dipping the ingredients in or a whole egg to add and try to cook and retrieve in one piece like a poached egg (use a spoon), or the egg can be added at the end and stirred round in the soup to break it up.

The Chinese Hotpot can be made with just meat or just fish or a combination. Use chicken or bone stock for white meats or a mixed meat and fish fondue, beef or bone stock for just red meats, and fish stock for a fish only fondue. A non-Chinese touch but a good one is to add a dash of sherry to the soup before serving.

Accompaniments

Boiled rice and soy or chilli sauce are the traditional ones but there is no reason why you shouldn't make your own version of this hot-pot by serving any of the sauces and accompaniments used for other fondues, see pages 33–35.

CHINESE HOTPOT

Quantities for 4.   Allow a total of 1½ *lb. meat and fish* (750 g.).

The meat should include *raw chicken* (breast is best);
fillet of pork; *beef fillet or rump*; *pig's kidney*; and *liver*.
Fish—raw fillets or cooked prawns
8 *oz. fresh vegetables* (250 g.)
Slivers of fresh ginger root (if you can't find this add ¼ *tsp.
ground ginger* to the stock)
1½–2 *pt. stock* (1 *l.*), *white or bone stock.*

Use enough to half fill the cooking pot, see page 44.

Soy sauce or chilli sauce   *Boiled rice*

The meat and raw fish should all be cut in small pieces, wafer thin, each kind arranged on a separate plate. The slicing is easier if the meat and fish are partially frozen.

The vegetables can be a mixture of roughly chopped Chinese cabbage or lettuce, small spinach leaves (stems removed), and dried mushrooms, each kind served on a separate dish. The dried mushrooms are prepared by soaking them in water for ½ hour or until they have doubled in size. Then remove the stalks and slice them.

The stock and ginger are brought to the boil in the cooking pot, then put on the table heater and kept bubbling.

Each guest has a plate, a dish of sauce, a bowl of rice, chopsticks and a wire ladle; also a bowl of Chinese tea.

Each guest chooses from the ingredients and puts the food in the cooking pot, using the wire ladle or chopsticks. After a couple of minutes or less, the cooked food is removed, the meat and fish dipped in the sauce and eaten.

When all the meat and fish have been eaten the soup is served in small bowls. Any vegetables left may be put in it and sometimes a raw egg may also be stirred in.

English Variations

Among the vegetables include diced aubergine or green peppers, pieces of young green beans, sliced peeled cucumber, tiny cauliflower sprigs, sliced fresh mushrooms.

Other meats may be included, for example veal or lamb.

Other sauces may be used in addition to the soy and chilli sauce, see page 34.

Instead of the Chinese wire ladle and chopsticks you can use small wire strainers, or a spoon and a fondue fork or wooden fondue sticks.

FONDUE CHINOISE (Swiss version)

Quantities for 4.

> 1–1½ *lb. lean fillet, rump or sirloin steak, well hung* (½–¾ *kg.*)
> 1½–2 *pt. well-seasoned chicken stock* (1 *l.*)
> 4 *Tbs. chopped parsley*   Soy sauce
> 3 *mayonnaise sauces,* see page 169–170
> 4 *egg yolks, very fresh and unbroken*   *French bread*

Have the beef sliced thinly in small pieces about 2 × 1 in. (5 × 2½ cm.), and arranged on a large flat serving dish or one dish between two.

Serve the parsley, egg yolk and sauces in small dishes, one portion of each per person. Provide a plate, dinner fork and fondue fork for each guest.

Heat the stock to boiling, bring to the table and keep hot, see page 44.

The egg yolk is used for dipping the meat in before cooking and the sauce and parsley after cooking. When all the meat has been eaten, the stock has fresh parsley added and is served as a soup, in small bowls.

CHICKEN HOTPOT, CHINESE STYLE

Quantities for 4.

1 *frying chicken or small roaster, about* 2½ *lb.* (1 *kg.*)

Remove the legs and wings and cut the meat from the breast in very thin slices. Similarly cut slices from the thighs and the rest of the bird until you have enough for four. The slicing is easier if the bird is partially frozen. Put the meat in the refrigerator until required. Put the carcase in the pressure cooker with water to cover and

1 *bay leaf*   4 *peppercorns*   2 *allspice*
Salt and pepper   *A piece of carrot*   *A piece of onion*

Bring to pressure and cook for ½ hr. Strain. When ready to serve the hotpot put a pint or more of the stock in the fondue pot, amount according to its size. Cut the thinly sliced chicken in small pieces suitable for spearing on forks and small enough to cook quickly. Arrange the meat on four small plates.

Accompaniments
Boiled rice; Soy sauce; Tartare sauce, see page 170; curry sauce, see page 174; watercress or other salad greens.

Serve a portion of these for each person.

When all the meat is eaten, serve the stock as a soup, in cups or soup bowls.

Alternative
Use four frozen chicken breasts instead of the whole chicken and make the stock with chicken cubes.

FISH HOTPOT CHINESE STYLE

Quantities for 4.   Allow 1½ *lb. fish fillets and shellfish, mixed* (750 *g.*)
For the fish use raw fillets of any fish, fresh or salt water. For shellfish

use cooked shelled prawns, sliced lobster tails, scampi tails, shelled fresh mussels or scallops.

8 oz. fresh vegetables (250 g.)
1½–2 pt. fish or chicken stock,
or fish stock plus some white wine (1 l.)

Use enough to half fill the cooking pot, see page 44.
The fish fillets should be cut in wafer-thin slices, easiest to do with half-thawed frozen fish.

To shell mussels, first wash them in several waters, scrubbing off as much sand and weed as possible. Put the fish in a large pan with a very little water, just enough to make some steam. Put the lid on and cook gently until all the shells have opened. Strain the liquid through muslin and add it to the fish stock. Remove the mussels from the shells and let them cool.

For the vegetables use sliced fresh mushrooms, pieces of young green beans, sliced peeled cucumber, diced green peppers.

Arrange each kind of fish and vegetable on a separate plate, or if you want to use fondue serving dishes put a selection of items on the plate.

Put the stock in the hotpot and bring to the boil, season well. Put the hotpot on the heater in the centre of the table and keep it bubbling.

Provide fondue forks, chopsticks, fish or table forks, or wire strainers for putting the food in, and removing it from the stock. The strainer is the easiest tool to manipulate. The fish needs only seconds in the boiling stock, vegetables longer according to taste; some like them crisp. The cooked fish is dipped in the chosen sauce and eaten with a fork.

When all the fish has been eaten, add any remaining vegetables to the stock and boil for a few minutes, then serve the stock in soup bowls with a spoon.

Accompaniments
Boiled rice; soy or chilli sauce; soy and ginger sauce, page 180; Tartare sauce, page 170; sour cream sauce, page 180; cold tomato sauce, page 180; cold curry sauce, page 174; pieces of anchovy fillet.

BEEF HOTPOT WITH RED WINE
Quantities for 4.

1–1½ lb. fillet or rump steak (½–¾ kg.)

Use the larger amount when buying rump steak with fat on it as you want only lean for the hotpot. Cut the meat in thin slices and make them thinner still by beating with a cutlet bat or wooden rolling pin. Cut these slices into bits about 1 in. by 2 in. (2½ by 5 cm.). Arrange the meat on lettuce leaves on individual plates or a larger one to share between two. The sauces can be put in a fondue dish or in small separate dishes.

¾ pt. canned consommé or good stock (400 ml.)
1 small peeled onion studded with cloves

Heat the stock or consommé in a fondue pot or other cooking pot, with the onion, and simmer gently until the onion and cloves have imparted some flavour to the stock.

¾ pt. red wine (400 ml.)

Remove the onion and add the wine. When it is bubbling transfer the pot to the burner or hotplate on the dining table and keep the liquid bubbling.

Provide fondue forks for use when cooking the meat and a knife and fork with which to eat it. The meat is cooked according to individual tastes and then dipped in the chosen sauce.

When all the meat has been eaten serve the stock as soup adding some chopped fresh herbs, if liked.

Suitable Sauces
Horseradish sauce, page 177; tomato ketchup; Worcester sauce; cold curry sauce, page 174; and any of the accompaniments listed on pages 33–35.

6 Fried and Grilled Meat and Fish Flambé

Flambé cooking in restaurants is very popular. It allows the waiter to show off, the customer to show off to other diners, and it usually, though not always, improves the flavour of the food. Doing a flambé in your own dining room costs only a fraction of what you would pay in a restaurant.

With many dishes the flaming is carried out at an early stage of the preparation and this may be followed by a fairly long cooking period in the kitchen. Here I am only concerned with flambé cooking in the dining room which is normally quite a short cooking process or a final flaming given to a dish which has been cooked in the kitchen.

The Apparatus
The traditional pans for flambé cooking are copper ones but many others are suitable including stainless-steel or aluminium frying pans, sauté pans or other shapes; also enamelled cast-iron and in some cases oven-proof ceramic or glass. When the entire cooking of the dish is carried out at table a metal pan is the most satisfactory to use as it heats up quickly, but when the food has preliminary oven baking before being brought to the table for its flambé, then any oven-proof baking dish is suitable. For foods which are cooked in the kitchen and then transferred to a serving dish, metal is the best to use, either stainless-steel or silver-plated.

Special apparatus is sold for flambé cooking, usually by the manufacturers of fondue sets. The equipment usually consists of a copper or stainless-steel sauté pan, oval or round, mounted on a trivet with one or two spirit burners below. Two burners are often necessary to give enough heat for frying. You can, of course, buy (from suppliers of catering equipment) the large spirit burners used in restaurants and then you only need one per pan. If you want to indulge in both flambé and fondue cooking you can buy the double burner with its stand and then use just one burner for the fondue pot and the two burners for flambé cooking. Sets of this kind are available complete with flambé pans and fondue pots.

When a dish has its preliminary cooking in the kitchen a moderate source of heat is enough to keep it hot for the flaming and a small spirit burner or even a candle warmer will suffice.

Alternatives to the special flambé apparatus, but not as elegant to look at, are an electric frypan, see page 10, or an electric hotplate, page 9. I find the frypan very good indeed for a flambé, especially useful because one can vary the temperature from very fast for frying to just keeping the food hot. With an electric hotplate you have a good range of heats and the advantage that you can use different sizes and kinds of cooking utensils for the flambé. Both these can be plugged in by a side table.

Flambé cooking should always be done on a side table well away from anything inflammable such as curtains, over-head light shades or people's hair and clothing. The flame shoots up high when the spirit is lighted so stand well back from the pan. If you are using a match to light it, avoid bending over the pan; stretch out your arm straight and keep your head well back. The same applies when you have set light to the spirit in a small pan or ladle as a preliminary to doing the flaming, stand back as you pour the lighted spirit over the food; this is when the flame will shoot up high.

Method
The actual method of carrying out the flambé will vary with the dish and in the recipes I have suggested appropriate methods. Foods with very little juice round them simply have the spirit poured over them and set alight, either by tilting the pan so that the flame sets it alight or by using a lighted match. A match always has to be used when the source of heat is electric or a candle warmer.

When a dish contains a fair amount of liquid or a sauce the spirit is usually heated separately in a spoon, ladle, or small pan, then set alight and poured flaming over the dish. The more liquid there is the more alcohol will be needed for a good flambé, otherwise the liquid will quickly douse the flame. Even when the spirit is poured over the food before being set alight a better flame is obtained if the alcohol is first warmed, but this is not essential.

In order to flame, the liquid used must have an adequate alcoholic content and this is why spirits such as brandy, rum, gin, vodka or

52

whisky are the usual ones, with liqueurs being commonly used for a flambé of sweet dishes and fruits.

The process of flaming burns up the alcohol and leaves just the flavour of the spirit or liqueur. If there is surplus fat in the sauce or round the food this will burn at the same time and the dish becomes less greasy.

While food to be finished à flamber is usually hot, cold food, and even ices, can be set alight by the technique of pouring lighted spirit over them.

Serving

For a successful flambé service you must have things organised so that warm plates are ready at hand and hot or cold accompaniments which go with the dish. A food warmer of some kind is a necessity. This may be a candle-heated warmer, a spirit-burner warmer, an electric warming plate or a separate heated trolley. On this will go plates and any hot sauces or vegetables to be served with the main dish; and the spirit can be warmed here too.

At the beginning of each recipe, I have listed the kind of heating required for the flambé with a reminder of other items you will need to have at hand for serving the completed dish.

FRIED FILLET OF BEEF FLAMBÉ

For this you need a good frying heat, either a large spirit burner, or a hotplate; or use the electric frypan. On the food warmer, have the plates, a dish of potatoes and the brandy to warm.

Cooking Time 3–6 mins. depending on the thickness of the steak and whether it is preferred rare or medium done.

Quantities for 4. Allow 1–1½ *lb. fillet steak* (½–¾ *kg.*), or 4 pieces.

Garlic clove   Salt and pepper   Clarified butter

Rub the steaks well with a cut clove of garlic and season them with salt and pepper.

When ready for cooking, heat enough butter to make a thin layer on the frying pan. When it is hot, 400° (200°C), put in the steaks and brown them quickly on both sides. Keep a good heat under the pan and continue turning frequently until the steak is cooked to taste. Avoid over-cooking or the meat will be tough and dry. Even when well-done it should still look plump and feel springy when pressed.

$\frac{1}{2}$ *oz. butter* (15 g.)   4 *Tbs. brandy*

Add the butter and when it has melted, add the brandy (preferably warmed), ignite and serve when the flames have died down.

Accompaniments
Straw potatoes or baked jacket potatoes; a green or mixed salad.

BARBECUED CHICKEN HALVES OR LEGS FLAMBÉ

This can be grilled in the kitchen and brought to the dining room for the flambé, or cook it on the side table. On the food warmer have plates, the spirit and any hot accompaniments.

Cooking Time $\frac{1}{2}$–$\frac{3}{4}$ hr.   *Quantities* for 4.

2 *poussin or small frying chickens or 4 portions of leg* (*thigh*) *from a frying or broiling chicken*

Cut poussin or chickens in half through the backbone and breastbone. The best way of doing this is to cut through the backbone with poultry scissors and then cut in half through the breast. The backbone may be cut out entirely. Wash and dry the chicken.

Make one of the basting sauces, recipes below, and brush or spoon the sauce over the chicken before starting to grill it. Cook it under a high heat to begin with, about 5 mins. each side or until well browned. Then reduce the heat and brush with more sauce. Continue cooking, turning often and brushing each time it is turned, until the chicken is cooked through. If in doubt, cut one by the top of the thigh to see.

Put the chicken on a hot metal dish and keep hot until ready to flambé.

3–4 *Tbs. warm brandy or other spirit*

Either ignite the spirit before pouring it over the chicken or pour over and then ignite. When the flames have died down, serve.

Accompaniments
Fried or sauté potatoes; a green salad; chicory and olive salad, page 184; orange and onion salad, page 187.

Basting sauces
No. 1

2 *Tbs. tarragon or other flavoured wine vinegar*
2 *Tbs. lemon juice*   2 *Tbs. olive oil*
$\frac{1}{4}$ *tsp. soy sauce*   *Salt and pepper*

Mix together and stir or shake before using.

No. 2

    1 *tsp. dry mustard*   2 *tsp. Worcester sauce*
    2 *Tbs. vinegar*   3 *Tbs. melted butter or margarine*

Mix together.

No. 3

    1–2 *Tbs. oil*   1 *tsp. salt*
    1 *tsp. curry powder*   *Pepper*

Mix well.

CHICKEN FLAMBÉ WITH CHERRIES

This is one to cook in the kitchen and keep hot until it is time to flambé it in the dining room.

The cooking can be done in an electric frypan or in a sauté pan. In the latter case serve the chicken on a heat-resistant dish which is really hot and flambé on the dish. On the food warmer have plates, the brandy, and any hot accompaniments, see below.

Cooking Time about $\frac{3}{4}$ hr.   *Quantities* for 4.

    4 *portions frying chicken*   1 *oz. butter* (25 *g.*)
    Seasoned flour

Wash and dry the pieces of chicken and coat them in seasoned flour. Fry them brown in the hot butter, 380° (190°C).

    8 *oz. red cherries* (125 *g.*) $\frac{1}{4}$ *pt. red wine* ($\frac{1}{2}$ *c. or* 150 *ml.*)

Stone the cherries and add them to the chicken, with the wine. Reduce the heat to 260° (130°C) and continue cooking, with the lid on the pan, until the chicken is tender. Most of the wine will have evaporated by the time the chicken is cooked.

    1–2 *Tbs. chopped fresh herbs*   *Salt and pepper*

Add to the chicken and keep hot until ready to serve.

    5 *Tbs. brandy*

Warm the brandy, ignite it and pour it over the chicken. Serve.

Accompaniments

Rice, noodles or potatoes and a green salad.

CHICKEN FLAMBÉ WITH CREAM

This can be cooked in an electric frypan and kept warm until the time comes to flambé and serve it, or cook it in an ordinary sauté pan or similar utensil; cover, and keep hot until ready to flambé it. If cooked in the frypan the flambé will be done in the pan; the sauté pan will have to be put on a large spirit burner or hotplate. On the food warmer you will need a hot dish to take the pieces of chicken while the sauce is being made, some plates, the brandy and any hot accompaniments, see below.

Cooking Time about 45 mins.   *Quantities* for 4.

   4 *portions of frying or broiling chicken*   1 *oz. butter* (25 *g.*)

If you are buying chicken pieces for this try to have them all the same, as this simplifies cooking. Heat the butter to a moderate temperature. Season the chicken and cook it in the butter until the outsides change colour but are not allowed to brown, 340° (170°C). Turn down the heat to 260° (130°C), cover the pan, and continue cooking more slowly until the chicken is tender. This will take less time for breast pieces than for legs, so remove the former as soon as they are cooked and keep them hot. When all are tender, return them to the pan to keep hot until required for service. If the chicken has been cooked in an electric frypan, plug this in at the side table with the control at 'warm'. A sauté pan will need to go over a spirit burner or hotplate.

   4 *Tbs. warm brandy*

Ignite the brandy and pour it over the chicken pieces, basting with the liquid. When the flames have died down remove the pieces to the hot dish you have ready. Keep hot.

   ½ *pt. double or sour or cultured cream* (250 *ml.*)

Add to the pan and stir well to incorporate the juices. Boil rapidly until the sauce thickens and is reduced by about half. Pour over the chicken and serve.

Accompaniments
Buttered noodles or new potatoes. Any vegetable you think appropriate or serve green salad.

Alternative
Before adding the cream sprinkle some paprika pepper into the pan or add some chopped fresh herbs to the cream while it is boiling.

CHICKEN AND MUSHROOM FLAMBÉ

This is cooked in the kitchen and then kept hot until the final flambé and serving. The cooking may be done in an electric frypan, or in a

56

sauté pan on the cooker. On the food warmer you will need plates, the brandy and any hot accompaniments, see below.

Cooking Time about 45 mins.   *Quantities* for 4.

2 poussin or 4 portions of frying chicken
1 oz. butter (25 g.)

Cut poussin in half through the backbone and breast-bone. Wash, dry and sprinkle with salt. Heat the butter in a sauté pan or in the electric frypan at 380° (190°C) and brown the chicken. Turn down the heat to 260° (130°C), cover and continue to cook until tender, 15–20 mins. Remove and put to keep hot.

4 oz. sliced onions (125 g.)
4 oz. whole small mushrooms or sliced larger ones (125 g.)
Salt and pepper

Add the onions to the sauté pan or frypan, adding a little more butter if necessary. Turn up the heat a little, 300° (150°C), and when the onions begin to soften add the mushrooms and continue cooking until the onions are tender. Sprinkle with salt and pepper.

2 Tbs. chopped fresh herbs (parsley, thyme, tarragon and marjoram)

Add to the pan and mix with the vegetables. Remove from the pan and put with the chicken.

¼ pt. dry white wine (½ c. or 150 ml.)

Put in the pan, and stir and heat until the sediment is dissolved.

1 tsp. potato flour

Mix smooth with a little cold water and stir into the wine. As soon as it thickens, return the chicken and vegetables and make sure they are hot before serving.

4 Tbs. warm brandy

The flambé may be done in the frypan, or the chicken served in a metal dish which should be very hot. Ignite the brandy and pour it over the chicken. Serve when the flames die down.

Accompaniments
Boiled rice or buttered noodles. Follow with a salad, see pages 183–7.

FLAMBÉ OF GRILLED LAMB CHOPS WITH LEMON AND GINGER MARINADE

Grilling can be done in the kitchen and the chops brought to the dining room for the flambé, or grill them on the side table. On the food warmer you will need plates, the spirit to warm and the hot vegetables.

Cooking Time 12–15 mins.   *Quantities* for 4.

> 4 *chump chops*   4 *Tbs. olive oil*   *Grated rind of* 1 *lemon*
> 2 *Tbs. lemon juice*   1 *Tbs. brown sugar*   1½ *tsp. ground*
> *ginger*   *Salt and pepper*

Put the chops in a single layer in a shallow dish. Mix the other ingredients together, stirring until the sugar is dissolved. Pour over the chops and leave to stand for 2–3 hrs., turning once.

Grill them under a moderate heat, turning occasionally and basting with the sauce. If you are not sure whether they are done enough, cut one through the middle. It should be just faintly pink in the centre by the bone.

> 3–4 *Tbs. warm brandy or other spirit*

Serve the chops on a hot metal dish and keep them hot until ready to flambé. Ignite the brandy and pour over the meat. Serve when the flames have died down.

Accompaniments
Creamed or fried potatoes; peas or green beans; mushroom salad, page 186; tomato and sweet pepper salad, page 187.

FLAMBÉ OF GRILLED LAMB CHOPS WITH HERBS

Grill in the kitchen and flambé in the dining room or grill on the side table. On the food warmer you will need plates, the spirit and any hot vegetables.

Cooking Time 15–20 mins.   *Quantities* for 4.

> 4 *loin chops or* 8 *cutlets*

Trim off any excess fat and put the cutlets on a large dish.

> ½ *tsp. powdered dry basil or rosemary*
> ½ *tsp. powdered marjoram*
> ½ *tsp. powdered thyme*   1 *tsp. salt*

Mix these together and rub it into both sides of the meat. Cover and store in the refrigerator for an hour. Grill under a moderate heat, turning frequently until the meat is brown and cooked, but just pink in the middle.

58

3–4 *Tbs. brandy or other spirit*

Warm the spirit. Serve the meat on a hot metal dish. Ignite the spirit and pour it over the meat. When the flames have died down, serve.

Accompaniments
Mashed or sauté potatoes; saffron rice, page 192; boiled carrots, cauliflower or onions in a Béchamel sauce, page 173.

MINUTE LAMB CUTLETS FLAMBÉ

This is for cooking on the side table using a frying pan on a good spirit burner or hotplate or use the electric frypan. On the food warmer you will need plates, the spirit and any hot accompaniments.

Cooking Time a few mins.   *Quantities* for 4.

8 *lamb cutlets from the best end of neck*
Garlic salt   Freshly-ground pepper

Carefully remove the 'eye' of meat from each cutlet. Flatten the meat out to about ¼ in. thick (½ cm.), using a cutlet bat or wooden rolling pin. Season with garlic salt and pepper.

1 *oz. butter* (25 *g.*)

Heat the frypan to 380° (190°C) and when it is up to temperature add the butter. In an ordinary frying pan, add the butter and heat until sizzling. Add the meat and fry quickly until brown on both sides.

3–4 *Tbs. warm brandy or other spirit*
1–2 *Tbs. lemon juice   Chopped parsley*

Pour the spirit over the meat and ignite. When the flames have died down, add the lemon juice and a little stock if needed. Stir and boil to incorporate all sediment in the pan. Add the parsley and serve.

Accompaniments
Creamed potatoes; rice with herbs, page 190; mixed green salad, page 185; brussels sprouts and celery salad, page 183; carrot and apple salad, page 184; chicory and orange salad, page 185.

FRIED FILLET OF PORK FLAMBÉ

A good heat is required for this so use either a large spirit burner, a hotplate or an electric frypan. On the food warmer you will need plates and any hot accompaniments, see below; also a hot dish to take the cooked pork while the sauce is being finished.

Cooking Time a few mins.   *Quantities* for 4.

1–1½ lb. fillet of pork (500–750 g.)

Mustard   Pepper   2 Tbs. oil

Remove any fat and fibres from the fillet and cut it in slices about ½ in. (1 cm.) thick. Season the slices with mustard and pepper. Heat the frypan to 360° (180°C), and when it is up to temperature add the oil. Then fry the pork quickly until browned and cooked through.

Salt   1 oz. butter (25 g.)   4 Tbs. brandy

Season the meat with salt, add the butter and allow it to brown. Then add the brandy and set it alight. When the flames have died down remove the meat to a hot serving dish and keep hot.

5 Tbs. white wine   ¼ pt. good stock (½ c. or 150 ml.)

Add to the pan and stir well to incorporate any sediment in the pan. Bring to the boil, season and pour over the meat as it is served.

Accompaniments

Noodles or potatoes; a salad, see pages 183–7, or vegetables such as green beans, young carrots or turnips or spinach.

GRILLED FILLET OF PORK FLAMBÉ

On the food warmer you need a metal dish for serving the meat, the spirit, plates and any hot accompaniments.

Cooking Time 20–25 mins.   *Quantities* for 4.

2 fillets of pork, total weight about 1–1½ lb. (500–750 g.)

Remove any fibres running along the outsides of the fillets. For this dish the fillets should be taken from the loin in one long piece. Fold under the thin ends and secure them with a cocktail stick or fine string.

Oil   A basting sauce, see pages 167–8

Brush the meat with oil and grill under a moderate heat or place several inches from the grill so that they cook through by the time they brown. During the second half of cooking, brush with the basting sauce to keep the surface moist. The meat is sliced before serving and this can be done before or after the flambé. Put it on a hot metal dish and keep hot until ready to flambé.

5 Tbs. warm brandy or other spirit

Ignite and pour over the meat, basting with the flaming liquid. Serve when the flames have died down.

Accompaniments
Sauté potatoes; buttered noodles; rice; green beans; peas; spinach; grapefruit and beetroot salad, page 185; orange and onion salad, page 187; tomato sauce, page 181; Espagnole sauce, page 175.

VEAL ESCALOPES FLAMBÉ WITH CREAM

This is meant to be cooked on the side table and for it you need a good frying heat such as that provided by a big spirit burner or a hotplate; or the electric frypan. On the food warmer you will need hot plates, the brandy and any hot accompaniments (see below).

Cooking Time a few mins.   *Quantities* for 4.

4 veal escalopes   *Salt and pepper*

Try to buy good veal escalopes, well beaten out, otherwise you will have to trim them yourself, removing any sinews and beating them out with a cutlet bat or a wooden rolling pin. Season with salt and pepper.

1 *oz. clarified butter* (25 *g.*)

If you are doing this in an electric frypan heat the pan at 320° (160°C). add the butter and when it melts add the veal. Melt the butter in a frying pan on a hotplate, or over a good spirit lamp, and when it is hot add the veal. Fry each side until it changes colour.

2 *Tbs. warm brandy*

Pour over the veal and ignite.

½ *pt. double cream* (1 *c. or* 250 *ml.*)
2 *tsp. tomato paste*
2 *canned red peppers, chopped*

When the flames have died down, add the cream and boil until it begins to thicken. Add the tomato and pepper, stir and heat for a few seconds and serve.

Accompaniments
Spaghetti dressed with some tomato paste and butter, buttered noodles or new potatoes. Spinach, green beans or peas, or salad.

FISH AND FENNEL FLAMBÉ

The fish is cooked in the kitchen and all you need in the dining room is a food warmer on which to put the serving dish, the plates and the spirit. A chauffe sauce is the best utensil in which to serve the melted butter sauce. Suitable for small fish like mackerel or red mullet, or a larger whole fish like hake or a smallish haddock.

Cooking Time 15–30 mins. depending on the size of the fish.
Quantities Allow ½–¾ lb. per portion (250–375 g.).

Whole fish   Salt and pepper

The fish should be cleaned, scaled, washed and drained, but head and tail are usually left on. Cut 3 or 4 gashes in either side and season with salt and pepper. Grill smaller fish and bake larger ones in a moderate oven. The fish should be placed on a wire rack such as a cake cooling rack, and cooked on the rack.

Dried fennel sprigs   Melted butter
Wedges of lemon   Boiled potatoes
1–2 Tbs. warm brandy or other spirit per portion

The fennel should be a bed of about 2 in. thick (5 cm.), placed on a stainless-steel serving dish or some other heat-resistant dish. When the fish is cooked transfer fish and rack to the serving dish, placing it on top of the bed of fennel. Ignite the brandy and pour it over the fish. This will ignite the fennel and when it has burnt out serve the fish with the melted butter, potatoes and lemon wedges handed separately.

Dried Fennel
Sprigs of dried fennel can be purchased from most herbalists, or you can dry your own, using ordinary garden fennel and drying the leafy sprigs in a warm oven.

FISH FLAMBÉ WITH TARRAGON SAUCE

The fish is cooked in the kitchen and served on a hot metal platter. A food warmer is needed when serving the fish and for the plates and potatoes, also to warm the brandy. The sauce should not be kept hot, only warm.

Cooking Time 15–20 mins.   *Quantities* for 4.

4 small fish (sea or fresh-water)

Each fish should be a suitable size for one portion. Use mackerel, trout, whiting or any fish available. Clean the fish but leave the heads and tails on. They can be grilled, baked in a moderate oven, or poached in simmering water with salt and a bay leaf. Avoid over-cooking. A fish weighing about 8 oz. (250 g.) will take 15 mins. to cook. While the fish is cooking, make the sauce.

5 *Tbs. milk*   *A good handful of fresh tarragon leaves*

Wash the leaves. Warm the milk in a small pan, add the leaves, cover and leave to infuse.

2 *egg yolks*   5 *Tbs. cold milk*
1 *tsp. potato flour*   1 *oz. butter* (25 g.)

Mix these together in the top of a double boiler or in a basin to go on top of a pan of simmering water. Heat, stirring all the time until the butter melts and the sauce thickens.

1 *oz. butter* (25 g.)

Add and stir until it melts and is blended into the sauce. Strain in the tarragon milk and add

1½ *oz. butter in small pieces* (45 g.)

Mix until this butter has been blended into the sauce.

Salt and pepper   *Lemon juice*

Season to taste. If the flavour of tarragon is not strong enough, put back the tarragon leaves and infuse longer, strain before serving. The sauce should be kept warm only, not left over the boiling water or it will spoil.

When the fish are cooked, remove the skin except from over the head and tail, and put them on a hot metal serving dish or oven-proof dish.

4 *Tbs. warm brandy*

When serving, pour the brandy over the fish, ignite and baste with the burning liquid. Serve with the sauce handed separately.

Accompaniments
Plain boiled potatoes are best.

PRAWNS OR SCAMPI FLAMBÉ WITH CREAM SAUCE

For this you need a frying pan on a moderate heat, such as a good spirit burner or hotplate; or use an electric frypan. On the food warmer you will want hot plates and the rice.

Cooking Time a few mins.   *Quantities* for 4.

2 *oz. butter* (50 g.)
12 *oz. cooked shelled prawns or scampi* (375 g.)

Melt the butter and heat the fish in it.

4 Tbs. brandy

Pour into the pan and give it a few seconds to warm up. Ignite and shake the pan.

Pepper   Grated nutmeg   2 Tbs. lemon juice

When the flambé dies down season the fish to taste.

½ pt. double cream (1 c. or 250 ml.)

Add to the prawns and simmer until the cream thickens.

Boiled rice, 8 oz. raw weight (250 g.)

Serve the prawns or scampi on a bed of boiled rice, garnished with parsley or other herbs.

PRAWNS OR SCAMPI FLAMBÉ WITH MUSHROOM SAUCE

For this you need a frypan on a moderate heat such as a good spirit burner, a hotplate; or use the electric frypan. On the food warmer you will need hot plates, the rice, the mushroom sauce and the brandy to warm.

Cooking Time a few mins.   *Quantities* for 4–6.

12 oz. shelled prawns or scampi tails (375 g.)
2 oz. butter (50 g.)

Melt the butter in the frying pan but do not allow it to become very hot. Add the shellfish and toss them until they are well heated.

4 Tbs. warm brandy

Ignite the brandy and pour it over the fish, basting with the liquid until the flames die down.

8 oz. (raw weight) of boiled savoury rice (250 g.), pages 190–2
Mushroom sauce, page 178

Put some rice on each dish, add a portion of prawns or scampi on top and pour over it some of the sauce; or hand the sauce separately.

Accompaniments
A salad to follow.

SOLE OR PLAICE MEUNIÈRE FLAMBÉ

With a large spirit burner, a hotplate or an electric frypan, this can be cooked entirely in the dining room. Otherwise cook the fish in the kitchen and bring it to a side table in the cooking pan or trans-

ferred to a heat-resistant serving dish for the flambé. On the food
warmer have the plates, potatoes, sauce if used, and the brandy
to warm.

Cooking time 8–10 mins.   *Quantities* for 4.

8 or more fillets of sole or plaice, according to their size
Seasoned flour   *1–2 oz. clarified butter (25–50 g.)*

Wash and dry the fillets and coat them with seasoned flour. Heat the
butter in a frying pan and cook the fillets over a good heat until they
are brown on both sides. Should you do small whole fish instead,
allow about 5 mins. each side.

8 oz. white grapes (250 g.)

Remove skins and pips. When the fish is cooked arrange the grapes
round it. Then take to the dining room.

4 or more Tbs. warm brandy

Pour over the fish, ignite and baste the fish with the liquid.

Accompaniments
Lemon wedges; boiled potatoes; mixed salad. If you want to add a
sauce serve Hollandaise, page 176, or lemon sauce, page 177.

7 Brochettes and Kebabs Flambé

These are ideal for the table-top grill or for the rôtisserie with its rotating spit, provided it has the equipment for holding kebab skewers, which most do. Kebabs are another last-minute cooking job, but you may prefer to do them in the kitchen though it is fun for others to see them cooking. They are also very popular for out-door cooking. For this you can supply a choice of ingredients and people can assemble their own skewers.

Brochettes, or cooking en Brochette, are the French names for bits of meat or fish, and vegetables, cooked on skewers, but in Eastern Europe and the Middle and Far East they are known by a variety of names which include Kebob, Kabob and Kebab—the different spellings used in Persian, Indian and Turkish cooking; Shashlik is Russian; Shish Kebab is the name used in Turkey for Kebabs served on a bed of rice.

It is important to have the right size and kind of skewer for these. They are supplied with some portable grills and rôtisseries. If you are using an ordinary horizontal grill or a horizontal spit roaster, the skewers should be square, not round. This is to hold the meat in position and prevent it from slipping around and cooking unevenly. Some table-top rôtisseries have an arrangement whereby the skewers are held vertically in a stand and the whole thing revolves in front of the grill; in this case round skewers are used.

Special square kebab or brochette skewers are usually about 10 in. (25 cm.) long in the shaft—which is satisfactory for most grills and rôtisseries—and one skewer of that size holds enough for one portion.

The only difference between cooking kebabs with an ordinary grill or cooking them on a rôtisserie is that the skewers have to be turned over by hand when grilling (once is usually sufficient), while in the case of the revolving spit the thing turns automatically.

In the recipes I have given guide-times but they may need adjusting with your particular piece of apparatus. Follow the manufacturer's instructions at the beginning and compare the times with mine. There is also, of course, the question of personal taste, whether you like things well-done or under-done. I like beef pink in the middle not raw; lamb and liver very faintly pink in the middle; other meats well-done: fish only just cooked through.

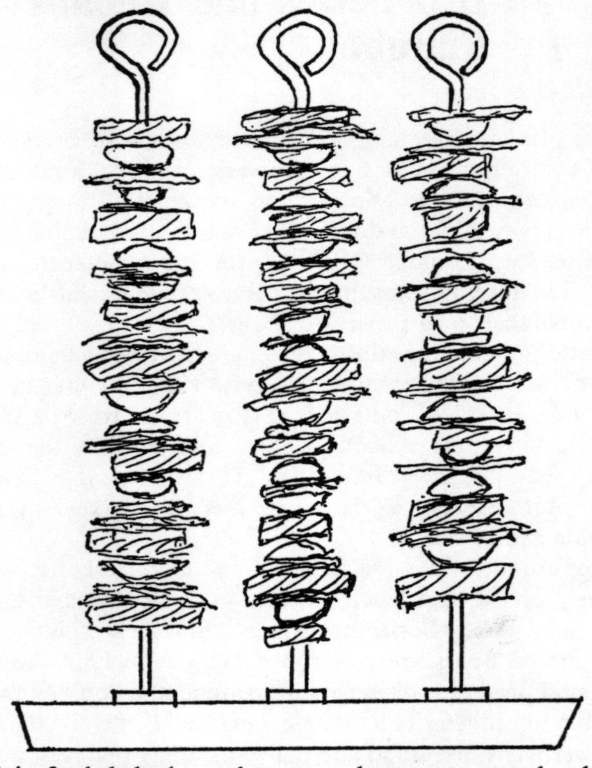

6. Spits for kebabs (meat, bacon, mushrooms, tomato, bay leaf).

If the meat being cooked is not in itself a fatty one, kebabs need basting with oil or a basting sauce, see page 167–8, and pieces of fat bacon are often threaded with the meat to act as basting devices.

The ingredients for kebabs can be prepared in advance and stored for an hour or so in the refrigerator, either on or off the skewers, and can be marinaded in the basting sauce to give them extra flavour.

To Flambé
On the food warmer you need the spirit, plates and any hot accom-

paniments. You also need a large metal serving dish, big enough to take the skewered food in a single layer. Have the dish hot and the spirit warmed, allow about 4 tablespoons for 4 portions. Use brandy, rum, whisky or other spirit. Set it alight, pour it over the meat and baste with the flaming liquid. When the flames have died down serve either on the skewers, or push the food off the skewers with the aid of a fork. Try to do this in a straight line so that it looks as it did when on the skewers.

If you prefer, any of these recipes can be served without the flambé and are very good, although they lack that extra flavour that only a flambé can give.

CHICKEN BROCHETTES FLAMBÉ

Cooking Time about 20 mins.   *Quantities* for 4–6.

> 4 *chicken breasts*   4 *rashers streaky bacon*
> 4–8 *oz. mushrooms* (125–250 *g.*)
> *Small firm tomatoes*
> *Slices of raw green pepper or slices of aubergine*

Cut the chicken in small pieces about $\frac{3}{4}$–1 in. wide (2–2$\frac{1}{2}$ cm.). Remove rinds from the bacon and stretch out the rashers with the back of a knife. Cut each in four or more pieces. Wash and drain the mushrooms and prepare the other vegetables, using those you prefer. You may want to blanch green peppers in boiling water to soften them. Thread the ingredients on skewers and keep them in a cool place until required.

> *Basting sauce*, see pages 167–8

Brush with the basting sauce, the basic one is very good with chicken. Grill gently until the bacon is crisp by which time the chicken should be cooked.

> 4 *Tbs. warm brandy or other spirits*

Serve the brochettes on a hot metal dish. Ignite the spirit and pour it over the chicken, basting with the flaming liquid. Remove from the skewers as you serve each one.

Accompaniments
Boiled or saffron rice, page 192.

The sauce can be one to pour over the brochettes when they have been put on a bed of rice; lemon sauce, page 177; Espagnole sauce, page 175; Hollandaise sauce, page 176. Alternatively, serve a cold sauce separately such as curry mayonnaise, page 169, or one of the other mayonnaise sauces, pages 168–170.

Follow with a salad, see pages 183–7.

CHICKEN LIVER KEBABS FLAMBÉ

Cooking Time 15–20 mins.   *Quantities* for 4.

8 oz. chicken livers (250 g.)   1 oz. butter (25 g.)

Wash and drain the livers and remove any fat or fibres. Heat the butter in a frying pan and cook the livers for a minute or two just to stiffen them. Remove from the pan and cut each liver into 3 or 4 pieces, depending on its size. Keep any butter left in the pan and use it for basting the kebabs.

8 *big, plump prunes*

Remove the stones, cutting the prunes in half. If they are not plump ones soak the prunes in water for a while to soften them.

4 rashers streaky bacon   *Salt and pepper*
Cayenne pepper   *Powdered dried rosemary or thyme*

Remove bacon rinds and stretch out the rashers with the back of a knife. Cut each in four pieces.

Thread the liver, prunes and bacon—alternating them—on the skewers. Season well and sprinkle them with the herbs and any butter left from frying the liver. Grill until the bacon is crisp.

4 *Tbs. warm brandy or other spirit*

Serve the kebabs on a hot metal dish, ignite the spirit, and pour it over the kebabs. Baste with the flaming liquid. Remove from the skewers as each is served.

Accompaniments
Boiled rice or saffron rice, page 192; green beans or a salad. They are pleasant without a sauce but if you prefer them more moist serve a savoury butter, page 170 or Béarnaise sauce, page 172.

FISH KEBABS FLAMBÉ

Cooking Time 15 mins.   *Quantities* for 4.

1½ lb. *fillet of halibut or other firm fish* (¾ kg.)

Wash and drain the fish, leaving the skin on. Cut it into pieces about the size of a walnut. Put the fish in a shallow dish.

70

1 *Tbs. oil* 2 *tsp. salt* 1 *Tbs. chopped parsley*
$\frac{1}{4}$ *tsp. pepper* 2 *Tbs. lemon juice*

Mix these in a small bowl. Then pour the mixture over the fish and put the dish in the refrigerator for $\frac{1}{2}$ hr. or so. This helps to make the fish firmer.

Fresh bay leaves

Wash, drain and cut large ones in halves. Thread the fish on skewers with a piece of bay leaf between each pair of pieces. Brush the kebabs with the remaining oil and lemon mixture and brush again once during cooking. Grill slowly until the fish looks opaque. Avoid overcooking, or it will be dry and lacking in flavour.

4 *Tbs. warm brandy or other spirit*

Serve the kebabs on a hot metal dish and pour the lighted spirit over them. Baste with the flaming liquid. Remove from the skewers as each is served.

Accompaniments

A green salad, and for a sauce serve Tartare sauce, page 170, lemon sauce, page 177, or Hollandaise sauce, page 176. French bread or rolls if required.

KIDNEYS EN BROCHETTE FLAMBÉ

Cooking Time 15–20 mins.   *Quantities* for 4.

4–8 *lambs' kidneys*

Cut these in $\frac{1}{4}$ in. slices ($\frac{1}{2}$ cm.) and remove the hard core.

4 *oz. button mushrooms* (125 g.) 8 *small tomatoes*
4 *or more rashers streaky bacon*

Remove rinds and cut the bacon in pieces. Thread the kidneys and other ingredients on the skewers, having a piece of bacon next to each slice of kidney. Put in a shallow dish while the basting sauce is prepared.

1 *tsp. dry mustard* 2 *Tbs. vinegar*
2 *tsp. Worcester sauce* 3 *Tbs. oil or melted butter*
Garlic salt   *Chopped fresh herbs*

Mix all together, pour over the brochettes and leave to stand until you are ready to cook them. Cook at high heat until the bacon looks cooked by which time the kidneys should also be done. Baste with the sauce two or three times during cooking.

4 *Tbs. warm brandy or other spirit*

Serve the brochettes on a hot metal dish.

Ignite the spirit and pour it over the brochettes. Baste with the flaming liquid. Remove from the skewers as each is served.

Accompaniments
Potatoes or rice; for a sauce serve Espagnole, page 175. Follow with a salad, pages 183–7.

LAMB KEBABS FLAMBÉ

Cooking Time 15–20 mins.   *Quantities* for 3–4.

1 *lb. of lean lamb from the top of a leg or use boned middle*
or best end of neck cutlets ($\frac{1}{2}$ *kg. boned*)

Cut the meat in $1\frac{1}{2}$ in. cubes ($3\frac{1}{2}$ cm.). The pieces should be as nearly equal in size as possible. Put them in a basin.

1 *small chopped onion*	$\frac{1}{2}$ *tsp. salt*
Pinch of pepper	2 *Tbs. lemon juice*
1 *bay leaf cut up*	1 *Tbs. red wine or cider*

Mix all together and pour it over the meat, cover and store in the refrigerator for 5–6 hours, or overnight.

6 *or* 8 *small firm tomatoes*   6 *or* 8 *small mushrooms*

Thread the meat on skewers alternating the pieces with mushroom or tomato. Grill until the meat is done to your taste

4 *Tbs. warm brandy or other spirit*

Serve the kebabs on a hot metal dish. Ignite the spirit and pour it over the meat. Baste with the flaming liquid. Remove from the skewers as each is served.

Accompaniments
Serve on a bed of rice or risotto, page 191, garnished with chopped parsley. Serve separately an Espagnole sauce, page 175.

FLAMBÉ OF LAMB KEBABS WITH CIDER BASTING SAUCE

Cooking Time 20–30 mins.   *Quantities* for 4.

1 *lb. lean, boneless lamb* ($\frac{1}{2}$ *kg.*)   1 *large onion*

Use either leg of lamb or boned middle or best end of neck. Cut the lamb in 16–20 pieces. Skin the onion and cut it in 8 pieces, separating the large layers. The onion will not cook through; it can be regarded as a means of flavouring and not eaten, or it can be parboiled before mixing with the lamb; cool it first.

Salt and pepper   2 tsp. ground ginger   2 tsp. dry mustard

Put the meat and onions on a large plate, sprinkle the flavourings on top and mix with the meat, rubbing in well. Cover the dish with foil, and put it in the refrigerator for several hours.

8 rashers streaky bacon   ¼ pt. dry cider (½ c. or 150 ml.)
4 Tbs. tomato ketchup

Remove the rinds and cut each rasher into 4 pieces. Mix the cider and ketchup. Thread the meat, bacon and onions on 4 skewers and brush with the cider mixture. Grill, brushing once or twice with the cider mixture.

4 Tbs. warm rum or whisky

Serve the meat on a hot metal dish, still on the skewers. Ignite the spirit and pour it over the meat, basting with the flaming liquid. Serve when the flames have died down. If there is any basting sauce left, this can be heated and poured over the meat before it is served.

Accompaniments
Rice; mixed green salad, page 185; green beans or peas; spinach.

FLAMBÉ OF LIVER KEBABS WITH FRESH SAGE LEAVES
Cooking Time about 20 mins.   *Quantities* for 4–6.

4 medium-sized onions

Skin and cut the onions in quarters. Separate the quarters into leaves and put them in a bowl. Pour boiling water over them and leave for a few mins. This will partly cook the onion, but the pieces will remain firm when cooked. If completely soft onion is preferred, parboil the pieces until they soften but are not flabby.

1 lb. calf or lamb liver (½ kg.)
8 oz. thin rashers bacon (250 g.)

The liver should be fairly firm for this, so, if you are using frozen liver, cook before it is completely thawed otherwise it will become too flabby to handle. Should this happen, stiffen the liver by frying it for a minute or so before cutting it in pieces. Cut it into about 36 pieces. Remove the bacon rinds and cut the rashers into 36 pieces.

3 doz. fresh sage leaves

Wash and drain the leaves. Put a leaf on each piece of bacon and fold this around a piece of liver. Thread these on skewers alternating with a leaf of the prepared onion. Grill until the bacon looks cooked.

4 Tbs. warm whisky or brandy

Serve the kebabs on a hot metal dish. Ignite the spirit and pour it over the meat. Baste with the flaming liquid. Remove from the skewers as each is served

Accompaniments

This is very good without a sauce, especially if the accompanying vegetables are moist or have a sauce with them. Alternatively, serve the kebabs on a bed of boiled rice and serve separately a sauce such as Espagnole, page 175.

FLAMBÉ OF MEAT BALL KEBABS WITH CHEESE

Cooking Time 20–25 mins.   *Quantities* for 4–6.

    1 *lb. lean, minced beef, or beef and pork mixed* ($\frac{1}{2}$ *kg.*)
    1 *large boiled potato, mashed or* 1 *portion mashed potato*
    *powder made up   *1 *tsp. salt   Pinch of pepper*
    $\frac{1}{4}$ *tsp. ground mace   *2 *oz. grated cheese* (50 *g.*)

Mix all the ingredients together using enough milk or water to make the mixture hold together. Shape into 20–30 small balls.

8 oz. small mushrooms (250 *g.*)
1 lb. small firm tomatoes ($\frac{1}{2}$ *kg.*)

Thread the meat balls on skewers, alternating with mushrooms and tomatoes. Grill until the balls are brown and cooked through.

4 Tbs. warm rum or whisky

Serve the meat balls on a hot metal dish. Ignite the spirit and pour it over the meat, basting with the flaming liquid. Remove from the skewers as each is served.

Accompaniments

Serve on a bed of boiled rice or Risotto, page 191, and accompanied by a green salad.

MIXED GRILL EN BROCHETTE FLAMBÉ

Cooking Time 10–20 mins. depending on the kind of meat and the size of the pieces.

Quantities Allow 4–6 oz. of mixed meats per person (125–175 g.) and 3–4 oz. vegetables and/or fruit (75–125 g.).

This can be made with the ordinary mixed grill ingredients, lamb, liver, sausage, bacon, beefsteak, kidney, tomatoes and mushrooms, or make your own choice from any of the following ingredients:

Meats
Beef steak (frying quality) cut in cubes or thin slices
Veal fillet, cut in thin slices
Lamb fillet, cut in cubes or thin slices
Pork fillet, cut in thin slices
Bacon rolls, thin streaky bacon (rinds removed), rolled up
Pieces of bacon, gammon or rashers
Lamb's kidneys, cut in half
Liver in thin slices
Chipolata sausages

Vegetables and Fruit
Tomatoes, small whole, or half larger ones
Mushrooms, fresh whole, button, or a little larger
Apple, cut in chunks
Banana, skinned and cut in 1 in. ($2\frac{1}{2}$ cm.) pieces
Sweet peppers, raw, in small pieces
Avocado pear, in slices

For brushing
Oil or a basting sauce, see pages 167–8.

Accompaniments
Rice with herbs, see page 190, or Risotto, page 191.
Baked beans
Chip potatoes
A sauce such as Espagnole, see page 175.
The pieces of food should be cut to sizes which will take about the same time to cook. Thread the pieces on skewers, alternating the meats with vegetables or fruit, or having several different meats together. Brush with oil or basting sauce before cooking and during cooking.

To Flambé
Allow 1 Tbs. warm brandy or other spirit per portion. Serve the brochettes on a hot metal dish. Ignite the spirit and pour it over the

meat, basting with the flaming liquid. Serve when the flames have died down. As each portion is served the meat is gently pushed off the skewer with a fork or, if you prefer it, serve on the skewers for guests to remove their own.

FLAMBÉ OF PORK AND PINEAPPLE KEBABS WITH CUMBERLAND BASTING SAUCE

Cooking Time about 30 mins.   *Quantities* for 4.

The Cumberland sauce may be made in advance, see page 174.

> *1–1½ lb. lean boneless pork, fillet is best but other tender meat will do (½–¾ kg.)*
> *1 lb. can pineapple cubes (454 g.) or use pineapple rings cut into pieces*
> *8 small, very firm tomatoes or 4 large*

Cut the pork in pieces about ½ in. square (1 cm.) or in thinner pieces if preferred; these will cook in less than 30 mins. Drain the pineapple. Wash the tomatoes and cut them in pieces a little bigger than the meat. They must be firm tomatoes, or they will overcook in the time it takes to cook the pork thoroughly. Thread the meat, pineapple and tomatoes on skewers, putting either pineapple or tomato between the pieces of meat. Brush with the Cumberland sauce, page 174, and grill, basting two or three times during cooking. The pork must be cooked right through. Heat the remaining sauce and serve it with the kebabs.

> *4 Tbs. warm brandy or other spirit*

Serve the kebabs on a hot metal dish. Ignite the spirit and pour over the meat, basting with the flaming liquid. Remove from the skewers as each is served.

Accompaniments

This is very pleasant as a dish on its own, but if you want to make it more substantial, serve the kebabs on a bed of boiled rice and spoon some of the sauce over it.

RUMP STEAK KEBABS FLAMBÉ

Cooking Time about 10 mins.   *Quantities* for 4.

> *1 lb. sirloin or fillet of beef steak (½ kg.)*
> *Salt and black pepper*
> *2 cloves of garlic or use garlic salt   Sugar*

Cut the meat in small cubes and sprinkle with salt and pepper. Rub this in and rub well with the garlic cloves or crushed garlic. If garlic salt is preferred use this in place of ordinary salt. Sprinkle with sugar.

2 Tbs. butter   2 small onions, finely chopped
Juice of 1 lemon   2 Tbs. sugar   1 tsp. soy sauce

Melt the butter, and lightly fry the onion until it begins to brown. Add the remaining ingredients and heat without boiling.

Thread the meat on skewers, put in a shallow dish and pour the sauce over it, basting to coat well, then grill.

4 Tbs. warm brandy or other spirit

Serve the kebabs on a hot metal dish. Ignite the spirit and pour it over the meat, basting with the flaming liquid. Remove from the skewers as each is served.

Accompaniments
Potatoes and a salad. If there is any of the basting sauce unused this can be served with the meat, otherwise serve a Béarnaise sauce, page 172.

SCAMPI BROCHETTES FLAMBÉ

Cooking Time about 45 mins. for the sauce, and a few mins. for the scampi.

Quantities allow 1½ pt. (1 l.) unshelled scampi tails for 4.

Scampi shells   1 bay leaf

Shell the scampi and put half the shells in a saucepan with water to cover and the bay leaf, and boil gently for 20 minutes to make stock. Strain.

2 oz. butter (50 g.)

Pound the rest of the shells in a mortar and gradually work in the butter. Rub through a sieve and set aside.

¾ oz. butter (1½ Tbs.)   ¾ oz. flour (2½ Tbs.)
8 fluid oz. fish stock (¾ c. or 200 ml.)

Melt the butter, add the flour and then the stock to make a sauce. Boil for a few minutes.

4 Tbs. white wine   5 Tbs. milk
5 Tbs. single cream   Salt and pepper

Add to the sauce and then gradually add the scampi-flavoured butter.
Keep the sauce warm.

8 *oz. rice* (250 *g.*), *boiled and flavoured with plenty of thyme,*
see Rice with Herbs, page 190

Cook the rice and keep it hot.

Lemon juice   *Melted butter*   *Pepper*

Sprinkle the scampi tails with lemon juice, brush them with melted
butter and sprinkle with freshly-ground white pepper. Thread on
skewers and cook for about 5 mins. or until they are really hot.

4 *Tbs. warm brandy*

Put the skewers of scampi on a hot metal dish. Ignite the brandy and
pour it over them, basting with the flaming liquid. As each portion is
served remove the scampi from the skewers onto a bed of rice, and
pour some of the sauce over them.

Alternative
If you have bought shelled scampi, instead of the above sauce use
Hollandaise sauce, page 176, or lemon sauce, page 177.

SWEETBREAD KEBABS FLAMBÉ

Cooking Time 5 mins. to blanch the sweetbreads; about 20 mins. to
grill.

Quantities for 4.

1 *lb. sweetbreads* ($\frac{1}{2}$ *kg.*)   *Lemon juice*

Soak the sweetbreads in cold water for about 1 hr. Then cover them
with fresh cold water, add a dash of lemon juice, bring to the boil and
simmer for 5 mins. Drain and cool enough to be able to handle them.

6 *oz. large mushrooms* (175 *g.*)   6 *rashers streaky bacon*

Wash, drain and cut the mushrooms in fairly thick slices. Cut each
bacon rasher into 4 pieces. Remove any membranes and fibres from
the sweetbreads, and cut them into pieces about the size of a walnut.

Thread the ingredients on skewers having a piece of bacon next to
each piece of sweetbread, so that it will be basted with the melting
bacon fat.

Oil or a basting sauce, see page 167

Brush the kebabs with oil or a basting sauce and grill until the bacon
is crisp.

4 Tbs warm brandy or other spirit

Serve the kebabs on a hot metal dish. Ignite the spirit and pour it over the meat, basting with the flaming liquid. Remove from the skewers as each is served.

Accompaniments
Hot curry sauce, page 175, is particularly good with this, but any other hot sauce may be used instead. Serve a hot green vegetable, or a salad, see pages 183–7; sauté potatoes, or boiled.

8 Omelets, Pancakes and Vol-au-Vents Flambé

All these are easy to cook à flamber. The omelets and pancakes are usually stuffed, but this is not essential, and it is usual to flambé after the filling has been put in—that is, at the final stage.

With vol-au-vents, the completed vol-au-vents are set alight, or the filling is made on the side table and it is this which has the flambé and not the pastry. I think to flambé the completed vol-au-vents is the simpler method for home cooking, but it does rather depend on the kind of filling, see the recipes.

With omelets, pancakes and vol-au-vents it is important not to use too much spirit, to ignite it before pouring it over the food, and to baste with the flaming liquid. The thing to avoid is having too much flame for too long, as that is liable to char this type of food and spoil the flavour.

More recipes for omelets and pancakes flambé are given among the Sweet Flambé recipes, pages 89–102.

CHICKEN LIVER OMELET FLAMBÉ

On the food warmer have plates and the spirit. If you are making the omelets on the side table have a hot metal serving dish heating as well. For cooking the omelets use a large spirit burner, or a hotplate.

Cooking Time About 5 mins. for filling and one omelet.
Quantities for one large or two small omelets.

4 *oz. chicken livers* (125 g.)   ½ *oz. butter* (15 g.)

Wash and drain the livers. Remove any fibres and cut the liver in small pieces. Heat the butter in a small pan and toss the liver in it for a minute, or until firm.

½ *Tbs. flour*   5 *Tbs. stock or wine*   *Salt and pepper*

Sprinkle the flour over the liver, mix and add the liquid. Stir until boiling and season to taste. Set aside to keep hot.

4 *eggs*   *Salt and pepper*   ½ *oz. butter* (15 g.)

Beat the eggs and add seasoning. Use a 7 in. (18 cm.) pan for one omelet to be divided in two when served. Heat the butter in the pan until it just begins to colour, add the eggs and cook quickly, lifting the edges to allow uncooked egg to run below. When almost set stop, leave to brown and when still slightly moist on top put the liver on the half away from the handle, fold over and tip onto the hot metal serving dish.

1–2 *Tbs. warm brandy or rum*

Ignite and pour over the omelet. Serve.

If preferred, two omelets can be made from this mixture, using a smaller pan; or the recipe can be doubled for 4. When cooking single omelets, slightly undercook the first ones so that they don't become over-done while being kept hot for the flambé. As each one is made, put it on the hot metal serving dish which you have on the food warmer, or, if you are doing the cooking in the kitchen, in the warming cupboard of your cooker.

MUSHROOM OMELETS FLAMBÉ

For this you need two small or one large spirit burner or a hotplate; a small omelet pan or a large frying pan 10 in. diameter (25 cm.); and a food warmer for the plates, the sauce and spirit, as well as for keeping the omelets hot if you are making four individual ones.

Cooking Time a few mins. provided that the Espagnole sauce has been made in advance.

Quantities for 4.

4–6 *oz. mushrooms* (125–175 g.)   2 *oz. butter* (50 g.)

Wash the mushrooms and slice them, stalks and all. Heat the butter in a small pan and cook the mushrooms for a few minutes.

8 *eggs*   1 *tsp. salt*   *Pinch of pepper*

Beat the eggs, add the seasoning and the cooked mushrooms.

1 *oz. butter* (25 g.)

The omelet can be made in one large pan or make four small ones. In that case, use a quarter of the butter for each one. Heat the butter, and when it just begins to change colour add the omelet mixture, making sure there is an even distribution of the mushrooms. Keep a good heat under the pan and stir the mixture well until it is beginning to set, then allow it to brown underneath and become almost set on top. Fold it over away from the handle and tip it onto a hot heat-resistant dish. Keep hot until all are made.

3–4 *Tbs. rum or brandy*   *Espagnole sauce* page 175

Warm the spirit and pour it round and over the omelets. Ignite it and serve. Hand the sauce separately.

Accompaniments
French bread or fresh rolls; a green salad.

STUFFED CHICKEN PANCAKES FLAMBÉ

A food warmer is all you require for this flambé. The pancakes are cooked and stuffed in the kitchen, kept warm on a metal dish, and brought to the side table for the flambé. Also on the food warmer should be plates and the spirit.

If you prefer, you can cook the pancakes at the side table; just make the batter and stuffing in advance. For cooking the pancakes you will need a strong spirit burner or a hot plate. The stuffing mixture should be kept hot on the food warmer and you will also need room on the warmer for the dish of completed pancakes, the serving plates and spirit.

Cooking Time 20–30 mins.   *Quantities* for 8 pancakes.

Filling

1 *oz. butter* (25 *g.*)   2 *oz. finely sliced mushrooms* (50 *g.*)

Melt the butter in a small pan, add the mushrooms, cover and stew gently for 3–4 mins.

2 *Tbs. flour* $\frac{1}{4}$ *pt. stock* ($\frac{1}{2}$ *c. or* 150 *ml.*)

Add to the mushrooms and mix well, then stir in the stock and stir until it boils.

4 *oz. diced cooked chicken* (125 *g.*)
2 *finely chopped hard-boiled eggs*
1 *tsp. chopped parsley*
1 *tsp. chopped tarragon*   1 *Tbs. cream*
Salt and pepper

Add to the mushrooms, seasoning to taste. Bring to the boil and then put over hot water to keep hot while the pancakes are made.

Pancakes

4 *oz. plain flour* ($\frac{3}{4}$ *c. or* 125 *g*) $\frac{1}{2}$ *tsp. salt*

Put in a basin and make a well in the centre.

2 eggs   ½ pt. milk (1 c. or 250 ml.)

Break the eggs into the middle and mix them gradually into the flour, adding milk gradually until half has been used. Then beat very thoroughly and add the rest of the milk. Pour into a jug.

Alternative method
Put all the ingredients in the goblet of the electric blender and process for 1 min.

Lard

Use a 7 in. (18 cm.) frying pan and heat it with a little lard in it. When hot, pour off surplus lard and put in a thin layer of the batter. Cook until brown underneath, turn or toss and brown the other side. Turn out on a piece of greaseproof paper, add a little filling, roll up and put in a hot metal serving dish (or a fireproof one). Put to keep hot. Make all the pancakes, filling in turn.

3–4 Tbs. rum or brandy

Warm in a small pan, ignite, pour over the pancakes and serve.

Variations
Substitute cooked veal, ham, game or other poultry for the chicken in the above recipe. Vary the herbs used according to the kind of meat.

PRAWN PANCAKES FLAMBÉ

Cooking Time 15–20 mins.   *Quantities* for 8 pancakes.

Pancakes
Make these in the same way as the recipe on page 83 for Stuffed Chicken Pancakes Flambé.

Filling

8 oz. shelled prawns (250 g.)   *¼ pt. sour cream* (½ c. or 150 ml.)
2 tsp. lemon juice   *Ground nutmeg*
Salt and pepper

Put all in a small pan and heat slowly to boiling.

2 tsp. potato flour   2 Tbs. sherry

Blend to a smooth cream and stir into the prawn mixture. Stir until it thickens and put to keep hot while the pancakes are made. As each pancake is finished turn it out onto a piece of greaseproof paper, put a spoonful of the filling on and roll it up. Put on a metal serving dish and put to keep hot.

1 *oz. melted butter* (25 g.)

When all are finished brush over with melted butter and put under the grill to crisp the tops.

3–4 *Tbs. warm brandy or rum*   *Lemon wedges*

Ignite the spirit and pour it over the pancakes. Serve with the lemon wedges handed separately.

CHICKEN VOL-AU-VENT FLAMBÉ

A flambé really does something for vol-au-vents. Make the pastry cases first and refrigerate them while preparing the filling. Then keep the filling hot in a double boiler while the pastry is baked. Keep this hot until the final assembling and flambé. If the dish is hot and the vol-au-vents hot there is no need to have any kind of heater.

Quantities for 4 good-sized vol-au-vents: for a main dish allow two each, otherwise one is sufficient.

1 *lb. puff pastry* (½ *kg.*), *home-made or ready-made*

This amount of pastry will allow you to cut all four vol-au-vents from the first rolling. The trimmings can be refrigerated or frozen and used later for a pie covering or sweet pastries.

Roll the pastry out to about ⅛ in. thick (3 mm.). Then lift it up from the board to let air get under and relax any stretching. Use a plain 3½ in. circular cutter (9 cm.) and cut out eight rounds. Put four of these on a baking tray. With a 2¼ in. cutter (5½ cm.) remove the centres from the remaining pieces. This size of cutter gives plenty of room for the filling. You can use a smaller one if you wish. Put the small pieces on a separate small baking tray. Brush the larger rounds with beaten egg and water or milk and stick the circles on top, being sure to have them on straight or they will topple over during cooking. Put in the refrigerator to chill.

½ *oz. butter or margarine* (1 *Tbs.*)   2 *Tbs. chopped green pepper*
3 *oz. drained and sliced canned mushrooms* (75 g.)

Heat the fat and cook the peppers and mushrooms in it for 5 mins., stirring frequently.

½ *oz. cornflour* (1½ *Tbs.*)   *Pinch of salt*

Add and blend well.

¼ *pt. milk* (½ *c. or* 150 *ml.*)
¼ *pt. chicken stock* (*or use mushroom stock*)

Add to the pan and cook until it thickens, stirring constantly.

> 1 *chopped canned red pepper*
> 6 *oz. diced cooked chicken* (1½ *c. or* 175 *g.*)
> *Pepper*

Add to the sauce, heat well, taste for seasoning and keep hot.
Remove the vol-au-vents from the refrigerator, brush with beaten
egg or milk and bake:

Temperature E. 450° (230°C) G.9 for 15–20 mins.

The small tops will be done in about 10 mins., so remove them first.

When ready to serve put the hot vol-au-vents on a hot fireproof
dish, add the hot filling, put on their lids and keep hot until ready to
serve.

> 2 *Tbs. warm brandy*

Ignite the brandy and pour it over the vol-au-vents. Spoon the flaming
brandy over them and serve.

LOBSTER VOL-AU-VENT FLAMBÉ

Make the vol-au-vent cases as described in the previous recipe up to
the stage when they are put in the refrigerator to chill. The filling
will be cooked on the side table so you simply need to assemble the
ingredients and tools for this.

Quantities for 4 vol-au-vents.

> 5–6 *oz. cooked or canned lobster meat* (150–175 *g.*)

If canned lobster is used, drain, keeping the liquid. Cut the large
pieces of flesh in slices and put the pieces on a dish. Refrigerate until
required.

> ½ *oz. butter* (15 *g.*)   1–2 *egg yolks*
> ¼ *pt. double cream*   2 *Tbs. brandy*

Put the butter in the frying pan you are going to use for cooking
the filling. Put the brandy in the chauffe sauce or other pan suitable
for warming it. Whisk the egg yolks into the cream and put in a
small jug or bowl. Refrigerate until required. Put the liquid from the
canned lobster in another jug or use a couple of tablespoons of fish
stock instead. Use 2 egg yolks if you like a thickish sauce.

About ½ hr. before serving the meal, bake the vol-au-vents.

Temperature E. 450° (230°C.) G.9, for 10 mins. for the caps and
15–20 mins. for the cases. Keep hot on a serving dish. When you are
ready for serving put this dish on the food warmer together with the
plates and the spirit.

86

Melt the butter and add the pieces of lobster cooking them gently until they are heated through.

Ignite the brandy and pour over the lobster. When the flames have died down add the fish stock and bring to simmering. Then add the cream and egg yolk and cook gently until the sauce thickens. Fill the vol-au-vents and put on the caps. If there is any surplus sauce pour this over the vol-au-vents.

Alternative

Instead of the lobster you can use crawfish tails or a mixture of cooked mussels and prawns, and some cooked button mushrooms can be included.

MUSHROOM VOL-AU-VENT FLAMBÉ

Make the vol-au-vent cases as described in the recipe on page 85, up to the stage when they are put in the refrigerator to chill. Finish as follows:

> *½ small onion, finely chopped*   *½ oz. butter (15 g.)*

Heat the butter in a small saucepan and fry the onion until it is just beginning to brown.

> *4 oz. mushrooms (125 g.)*   *½ oz. flour (1½ Tbs. or 15 g.)*

Wash mushrooms and chop coarsely. Add to the onion and mix. Mix in the flour and cook for a minute or two.

> *¼ pt. chicken stock (½ c. or 150 ml.)*

Add and stir until it boils.

> *2 oz. shelled walnuts (50 g.)*
> *Chopped fresh herbs or powdered dry herbs*
> *Garlic salt   Salt and pepper*

Chop the walnuts coarsely and add to the pan. Season to taste

> *2 Tbs. sour cream*

Mix in and put the filling to keep hot until ready to serve the vol-au-vents.

Remove the vol-au-vents from the refrigerator, brush with beaten egg or milk and bake:

Temperature E. 450° (230°C) G.9 for 15–20 mins.

The small tops will be done in about 10 mins., so remove them first.

When ready to serve put the hot vol-au-vent cases on a hot metal dish, add the hot filling, put on the lids and keep hot until ready to serve, but avoid keeping them too long as the filling tends to make the pastry soggy.

2 Tbs. warm brandy or other spirit

Ignite the spirit and pour it over the vol-au-vents. Spoon the flaming liquid over them and serve.

SHELLFISH VOL-AU-VENT FLAMBÉ

Make the vol-au-vent cases as described in the recipe on page 85 up to the stage when they are put in the refrigerator to chill. Finish as follows:

1 oz. butter (25 g.) 1 small onion, chopped
1 small green pepper, chopped

Heat the butter in a small pan and fry the vegetables in it until the onion is soft.

½ oz. flour (1½ Tbs.)

Add and mix in well, cooking for a few seconds.

8 oz. can of peeled tomatoes (226 g.)
1 tsp. chopped fresh marjoram
Salt and pepper ½ tsp. sugar

Mix until it boils and then simmer for 15 mins.

5 Tbs. white wine 4 oz. shelled prawns, crab or lobster (125 g.)

Add to the sauce and keep hot while the vol-au-vents are cooked.

Remove the vol-au-vents from the refrigerator, brush with beaten egg or milk and bake.

Temperature E. 450° (230°C) G.9. for 15–20 mins.
The small tops will be done in about 10 mins., so remove them first.

When ready to serve put the hot vol-au-vent cases on a hot heat-resistant dish, add the hot filling, put on the lids and keep hot until ready to serve but avoid keeping too long as the filling tends to make the pastry soft.

2 Tbs. warm brandy or other spirit

Ignite the brandy and pour it over the vol-au-vents. Spoon the flaming spirit over them and serve.

9 Flambé Sweets

These make an unusual and interesting hot fruit course, very pleasant at the end of the meal. The fruits need to be fairly firm ones which won't become mushy with cooking. Cut them in pieces of approximately equal size so that they will cook evenly.

I have given three examples in the following recipes; they can be varied to suit individual tastes. The cooking times given are for a spit roaster, but the kebabs can be cooked under an ordinary grill, turning them at half time. It is better to cook them fairly slowly or the edges may burn.

Fruit kebabs can be kept hot for some time in a warming cupboard so if you don't want to cook them on the side table cook them in the kitchen before the meal is served.

Rum or a liqueur are the best spirits for this kind of flambé. Allow about 1 tablespoon for each portion and have the spirit warm. Put the kebabs on their skewers on a hot metal serving dish, ignite the spirit and pour it over the fruit, basting with the flaming liquid. When the flames have died down serve, by removing from the skewers with the aid of a fork. They can be served with or without cream, or can be used as a garnish for other sweets, for example, ice cream.

For general notes on kebab cooking, see page 67.

BANANA KEBABS FLAMBÉ

Cooking Time about 10 mins.
Quantities Allow 1–2 bananas per portion.

Bananas   2 *Tbs. rum or liqueur for 4 bananas*

Skin the bananas and prick them all over with a fork. Cut each across into two pieces and roll them in the rum or liqueur to coat them all over. Leave for about 15 mins. for the spirit to soak in.

Melted butter   Caster sugar

Brush the bananas with the butter. Put some sugar on a piece of greaseproof paper and roll the bananas in the sugar. Thread them on skewers lengthwise, and grill until they are tender. They can be cooked in advance and kept warm.

1 Tbs. warm rum or liqueur per portion (the same kind as used for soaking)   Wedges of lemon   Cream

Serve the bananas on a hot metal dish, having previously removed the skewers. Ignite the spirit and pour it over the bananas, basting with the flaming liquid. When the flames have died down serve with a choice of lemon or cream.

DRIED FRUIT KEBABS FLAMBÉ

Cooking Time 15–20 mins.   Quantities for 4.

4 oz. dried apricots (125 g.)   4 oz. plump prunes (125 g.)
1 or 2 oranges   4 oz. canned pineapple chunks (125 g.)

Soak the apricots in cold water for an hour or so and then drain. Stone the prunes and drain the pineapple. Just before cooking the kebabs peel the oranges, cut across in $\frac{1}{2}$ in. thick slices (1 cm.). Cut the slices in two or three pieces depending on their size. Thread the fruit on skewers alternating the various kinds.

2 Tbs. honey   4 Tbs. lemon juice

Mix these until the honey dissolves and use the mixture to brush the fruit before cooking and again during cooking. Serve the fruit on the skewers on a hot metal dish.

4 Tbs. warm rum or liqueur   Single cream or whipped cream

Ignite the spirit and pour it over the fruit, baste with the flaming liquid. Remove from the skewers as it is served. If there is any honey basting liquid left, pour this over the fruit. Hand the cream separately.

FRESH FRUIT KEBABS FLAMBÉ

Cooking Time 15–20 mins.   Quantities for 4.

2 firm bananas   2 medium-sized oranges
2 or more dessert apples

The apples may be prepared in advance and kept submerged in cold water but prepare the other fruit as near to cooking time as possible.

Wash the apples, cut in quarters, remove cores and cut each wedge in half. Skin the bananas and cut them in 1 in. pieces (2½ cm.). Peel the oranges and cut across in ½ in. thick slices (1 cm.) and then cut each slice in 2 or 3 pieces depending on the size.

2 Tbs honey   4 Tbs. orange juice   Pinch of ground cinnamon

Mix together until the honey dissolves. Thread the fruit on skewers and brush with the orange juice mixture. Cook until the apples are tender, brushing again during cooking.

4 Tbs. warm rum or liqueur   Single or whipped cream

Serve the kebabs on a hot metal dish. Ignite the spirit and pour it over the fruit, basting with the flaming liquid. Remove the fruit from the skewers as it is served. If there is any honey basting liquid left pour it over the fruit. Hand the cream separately.

APPLES FLAMBÉ

This is for cooking in the kitchen and keeping warm until required. A food warmer gives sufficient heat for the flambé.

Cooking Time about 30 mins.   *Quantities* for 4.

4 oz. sugar (½ c. or 125 g.)   ½ pt. water (1 c. or 250 ml.)

Heat together until the sugar has dissolved and the syrup boiling.

4 medium-sized cooking apples   Vanilla essence

Peel and core the apples. Add vanilla to the syrup to taste and poach the apples in this, turning them frequently until they are tender but not broken. Lift them into a hot metal dish or individual metal dishes. Keep hot. Boil the syrup rapidly to reduce and thicken it and pour over the apples. Put to keep warm during the service of the rest of the meal.

3–4 Tbs. warm rum

Ignite the rum, pour it over the apples and serve while they are flaming; they are especially attractive when they are in individual dishes.

Whipped or single cream

Hand the cream separately.

APRICOTS FLAMBÉ

Only a moderate heat is needed for this, such as a good spirit burner, but a hotplate or electric frypan is also suitable.

Cooking Time a few mins.   *Quantities* for 3–4.

1 lb. can of apricot halves (454 g.)

Drain the fruit thoroughly.

½ oz. butter (1 Tbs.)   1 Tbs. caster sugar

Melt the butter, add the sugar and allow it to dissolve. Add the fruit and turn it over in the butter and sugar mixture until it is coated and hot.

4 Tbs. warm rum

When the fruit is hot add the rum and ignite or ignite the rum first. Baste the fruit with the sauce and serve.

Single cream

Hand this separately.

FRIED BANANA FLAMBÉ

Frying heat is required, so use a large spirit burner, a hotplate or an electric frypan.

Cooking Time a few mins.   *Quantities* for 4.

2 oz. butter (50 g.)   4 large or 8 small bananas
4 Tbs. rum, brandy or other spirit   Granulated sugar

Peel the bananas just before use and leave small ones whole but cut large ones in half lengthwise. Fry them for a few minutes in the hot butter, turning once. Pour on the spirit, ignite it and sprinkle the fruit with sugar. Baste with the liquid and serve.

Accompaniments
Lemon wedges for those who like sharpness; cream for the others.

GRILLED BANANA FLAMBÉ

These can be cooked in the kitchen and kept warm until required, or cook them on the side table if you have a grill installed there. On the food warmer have plates and the spirit to warm.

Cooking Time 5–10 mins.   *Quantities* for 4.

4 large ripe bananas or 8 small ones   1 oz. butter (25 g.)

Melt the butter. Skin the bananas and brush them all over with butter to coat completely. This may be done in advance of cooking as the butter coating prevents the bananas from discolouring.

92

Put them in the bottom of a solid grill pan (not on a rack), or in a metal dish suitable for putting under the grill. A stainless-steel dish in which they can be served is ideal for this. Grill under a moderate heat until the bananas are lightly browned on both sides; use tongs for turning them. At this stage they may be put to keep warm until required.

3 Tbs. warm rum or brandy   1 Tbs. caster sugar

¼–½ pt. thick cream (½–1 c. or 150–250 ml.)

Take these into the dining room with the hot bananas. Pour the rum or brandy over the bananas, ignite, sprinkle with the sugar and baste with the burning liquid. When the flame has died down pour the cream over the bananas and serve.

PEACHES WITH KIRSCH FLAMBÉ

Frying heat is required, so use either a large spirit burner, a hotplate or an electric frypan.

Cooking Time 10–15 mins.   *Quantities* for 4.

4 large ripe peaches

Skin the peaches by putting them in a bowl and pouring in boiling water to cover. Leave for a minute. Pour off the hot water, add cold and the peaches should peel easily. They may be skinned in advance and kept in a bowl of cold water with a saucer on top of the fruit to keep it submerged.

2 oz. butter (50 g.)   1½ oz. caster sugar (3 Tbs).

1 Tbs. lemon juice

Heat the butter in a frying pan. Add sugar and lemon juice. Cook the peaches in this, rolling them about or basting them frequently until the sugar has caramelised a little.

2 Tbs. kirsch

Add to the pan. Ignite and serve while flaming.

Accompaniments
None really necessary, but serve cream for those who want it.

CANNED PEARS FLAMBÉ

As the pears don't require any cooking this flambé can be done over a moderate heat, for example, a good spirit burner; or use an electric frypan.

93

Quantities for 4.

8 *halves of canned pears*

Empty into a strainer and leave for a while to drain very thoroughly. Then put them on a dish and assemble the other ingredients required for the flambé.

½ *oz. butter* (15 g.)   4 *Tbs. warm rum*
1 *Tbs. fine brown sugar*

Use a small frying pan or the electric frypan and melt the butter. Add the pears and turn them over carefully, using a spoon and fork, until they are coated with butter and warmed through. Ignite the rum, pour it over the fruit and sprinkle with the sugar. Serve.

Accompaniments
Cream is optional. Chopped toasted almonds can be served separately for sprinkling over the pears.

RAW PEARS FLAMBÉ

Frying heat is required, so use either a small frying pan on a large spirit burner or hotplate, or use an electric frypan.

Cooking Time 10–15 mins.   *Quantities* for 4.

4 *ripe pears*   2 *Tbs. rum*

Peel the pears, halve and core and put them on a flat dish. Spoon the rum over them, turning to coat them well. Prepare the other items for the flambé.

1 *oz. butter* (25 g.)   2 *oz. caster sugar* (4 *Tbs.* or 50 g.)

Heat the butter, add the sugar and cook gently, without stirring, until it turns a pale caramel colour. Turn down the heat. Add the pears and turn and cook them, basting with the sauce.

3–4 *Tbs. warm rum*   2 *Tbs. orange or lemon juice*

Add the rum to the pears and ignite. Baste with the flaming sauce. Add the fruit juice and stir to dissolve any caramel remaining. Serve the pears with the sauce poured over them.

Accompaniments
Single or whipped cream handed separately.

FLAMBÉ PEARS WITH CHOCOLATE ICE CREAM

For the flambé use a small frying pan on a good spirit burner or hotplate, or use an electric frypan.

94

8 halves of canned pears

Tip these into a strainer and leave to drain. Assemble the other ingredients.

4 portions chocolate ice cream

Put these in a bowl embedded in crushed ice or put the ice cream in a vacuum container. This should keep the ice cream from melting while the pears are flamed.

½ oz. butter (15 g.) 4 Tbs. warm rum
1 Tbs. fine brown sugar

Melt the butter. Add the pears and turn them over carefully, using a spoon and fork, until they are coated with butter and warmed through. Pour the rum over the fruit, ignite and sprinkle with the sugar.

Put a portion of ice cream in each dish (metal or heat-resistant glass for safety), add the pears and any liquid in the pan.

Chopped toasted almonds

Sprinkle over the pears and serve.

PINEAPPLE FLAMBÉ

Frying heat is required for this, so use either a large spirit burner, a hotplate or an electric frypan.

Cooking Time about 10 mins. *Quantities* for 4–6.

8–12 small slices of fresh or canned pineapple
Kirsch (about 2 Tbs.)

Drain the canned pineapple thoroughly. Peel the fresh pineapple. Put the fruit on a large flat dish and pour a little kirsch over it.

1 oz. butter (25 g.) 2 oz. caster sugar (4 Tbs.)

Use a frying pan and heat the butter in it. Add the sugar and cook gently without stirring until it turns a pale caramel colour. Add the fruit and cook to heat it, basting with the sauce.

About 3 Tbs. rum or brandy or liqueur to taste
2 Tbs. orange juice (or lemon juice for a sharper flavour)

Add the spirit and set it alight. When it has burned out add the orange or lemon juice and serve the fruit with a little sauce poured over it. Cream may be served with it but it is usually preferred without.

PINEAPPLE FLAMBÉ WITH VANILLA ICE CREAM

Frying temperature is required, so use either a large spirit burner, a hotplate or an electric frypan.

Quantities for 4.

4 *large rounds of pineapple, fresh or canned*
About 1 *Tbs. kirsch*

Drain canned pineapple thoroughly, prepare fresh by peeling and removing any hard central core. Put the pineapple in a shallow dish and pour the kirsch over it.

4 *portions of vanilla ice cream*

The ice cream portions can be prevented from melting while the flambé is being made, if you put them in a metal bowl and embed this in crushed ice in another bowl; or use a vacuum container for the ice cream. Assemble the ingredients for the flambé and have them on a side table or trolley.

1 *oz. butter* (25 *g.*)   2 *oz. caster sugar* (4 *Tbs. or* 50 *g.*)

Melt the butter in a frying pan large enough to take the 4 pieces of pineapple. Add the sugar and cook until it melts, but don't stir. Put in the fruit and turn it over, basting with the sauce.

3 *Tbs. rum, brandy or liqueur*
2 *Tbs. orange or lemon juice*

Add the spirit and set it alight. When it is burnt out, add the fruit juice and mix in. Put the fruit in heat-resistant serving dishes, put a portion of ice cream on each and pour any remaining liquid in the pan, over the ice cream. Serve at once.

BANANA PANCAKES FLAMBÉ

These are for cooking in the kitchen. Keep them warm on a metal dish until ready to serve them. On the food warmer have plates, the dish of pancakes, and rum.

Cooking Time about 20 mins.   *Quantities* for 4.

4 *bananas*   *Lemon juice or sugar*

Peel and mash the bananas with a fork. Add lemon juice to taste if you like something sharp, or sugar if you think the bananas are not sweet enough.

2 eggs
4 oz. plain flour ($\frac{3}{4}$ c. or 125 g.)
1 oz. caster sugar (2 Tbs. or 25 g.)
$\frac{1}{2}$ pt. milk (1 c. or 250 ml.)

Put the flour and sugar in a mixing bowl and make a well in the centre. Add the eggs. Begin mixing from the centre and work in the flour, adding milk to make a smooth batter. When half the milk has been added beat the batter thoroughly. Add remaining milk and pour the batter into a jug.

Lard

Heat a 7 in. frying pan (18 cm.) with a little lard. When it is hot pour out any surplus lard and add a thin layer of the pancake batter. Cook until brown underneath, turn or toss and brown the other side. Turn out on a piece of greaseproof paper, add a little of the mashed banana, roll up, and put on a hot metal serving dish. Keep hot. As each pancake is made add it to the others. Keep hot until ready to serve.

4 Tbs. rum   Caster sugar

Warm the rum, ignite it and pour over the pancakes. Sprinkle with caster sugar and serve with

Lemon wedges

CRÊPES SUZETTE

This is one of the pancake recipes that must be finished at the last moment and is pleasant for guests to watch. You will need either a spirit lamp or an electric hotplate on a side table or trolley. An electric frypan can also be used. The pancakes can be made in advance and kept warm, or allowed to become cold in which case they will need a little longer in the sauce before they are served. Have serving plates on the food warmer.

Cooking Time 15–20 mins. for the pancakes; a few mins. for finishing.
Quantities for 8–10 pancakes about 7 in. diameter (18 cm.).

4 oz. plain flour (125 g.)   1 oz. caster sugar (2 Tbs. or 25 g.)
2 eggs $\frac{1}{2}$ pt. milk (1 c. or 250 ml.)

Put the flour and sugar in a basin, make a well in the centre, drop in the egg, add a little milk and mix from the centre gradually working in the flour. When half the milk has been added beat well and then add the remaining milk.

Alternative method: Put all ingredients in a blender and mix for 1 minute.

Pour the mixture into a jug.

Heat a little lard in a 7 in. (18 cm.) frying pan, and when it is hot pour out any surplus lard, leaving just a greasing on the surface . . . Pour in enough batter to make a thin coating on the bottom of the pan. The thinner they are the nicer they will be. Brown underneath, turn or toss and brown the other side. Turn out on a flat plate and keep warm or leave to cool. Add more lard as it seems necessary for cooking the rest. As they are done, pile them on top of one another, keeping them flat.

> *2 oz. butter (50 g.)   2 oz. caster sugar (4 Tbs. or 50 g.)*
> *The very finely-grated zest of 1 orange   1 Tbs. orange juice*
> *3 Tbs. curaçao or cointreau   3–4 Tbs. brandy or rum*

Assemble these ingredients on a tray for the finishing process. The same pan can be used. Have matches at hand, hot plates for serving and a table spoon and fork. The butter can be put in the pan. Have the sugar in a small dish and the orange rind, and juice and the curaçao or cointreau in a small jug (foil-covered if being kept a while). Measure out the brandy or rum into another small jug and cover it.

When the time comes to serve the Crêpes Suzette, fold each one in four to make a triangle and arrange them on a dish. Heat the butter to melt it. Add the sugar and stir until it bubbles, then add the orange mixture and when this is bubbling put in the folded pancakes and baste and turn them until they are well coated with sauce and it has almost all been absorbed. Add the brandy or rum, ignite and serve.

LAYERED ORANGE PANCAKES FLAMBÉ

These are cooked in the kitchen and kept hot on a metal dish. On the food warmer have plates, the rum, and eventually the dish of pancakes.

Cooking Time about 20 mins.   *Quantities* for 4.

> *2 large oranges or two 11 oz. cans mandarin oranges (2 × 312 g.)*
> *2 Tbs. rum, cointreau or curaçao.*

Peel fresh oranges and cut in thin slices removing all pith and pips. Cut the slices in small pieces and put in a shallow dish with the rum or liqueur. Add a little sugar if the oranges seem sharp. Leave to stand.

4 oz. plain flour (¾ c. or 125 g.)
1 oz. caster sugar (2 Tbs. or 25 g.)
2 eggs   ½ pt. milk (1 c. or 250 ml.)

Put the flour and sugar into a basin. Make a well in the centre and add the eggs. Mix from the centre, gradually working in the flour and adding milk to give a smooth batter. When half the milk has been used beat the batter very thoroughly, add remaining milk and pour the batter into a jug.

Alternative method: Put all ingredients in the electric blender and mix for 1 min.

Lard

Heat a very little in a 7 in. frying pan (18 cm.). When it is hot, pour out any surplus and add enough batter to make a thin film on the surface. Cook until brown underneath, turn or toss and brown the other side. Turn out flat on a hot dish. Put to keep warm. As the pancakes are made, pile them up and keep warm until required for serving. Then layer them in a pile on a hot metal dish with the fruit between layers. Sprinkle the top with caster sugar.

4 Tbs. warm rum

Take the pancakes and rum to the side table or on a trolley. Ignite the rum and pour it over the pancakes. Baste with the flaming rum and when the flame has died down, cut the pancake pile in wedges like a cake.

Whipped cream

Hand separately.

MERINGUE GLACÉ FLAMBÉ

No special heating arrangements needed for this.

Quantities for 4.

This can be made with ordinary confectioner's meringues, but I prefer to make my own, flavoured with coffee, and to fill them with a chocolate or mocha ice cream.

Coffee Meringues

Cooking Time 2 hrs. or more.   *Temperature* E. 250–275° (120–140°C)
G. ¼–½.

2 egg whites   4 oz. granulated sugar (½ c. or 125 g.)
1–1½ tsp. soluble coffee

Beat the egg until it is stiff enough to stand up in peaks and begins to look grainy. Add half the sugar and the coffee powder and beat until the mixture is very thick. Fold in the remaining sugar. Put in 8 spoonfuls on baking trays covered with non-stick paper or foil. Bake until they are completely dry. Allow to cool and store in an air-tight container.

Serving
Use metal serving dishes and put two meringues in each, sandwiched with a good portion of chocolate ice cream.

4 Tbs. rum, warmed

Ignite the rum and pour some over each portion while the spirit is still flaming. Serve at once.

Variations
Omit the coffee from the meringue recipe and sandwich the pairs of meringues with any ice cream to taste, varying the spirit according to the flavour; for example, use orange ice cream and curaçao for the flambé; banana ice cream and rum: raspberry ice cream and fromboise: coffee ice cream and brandy.

SAVARIN FLAMBÉ

You can use ready-made Savarin or babas but the home made is usually nicer and it is easy to make. The mixture can be cooked in a Savarin or border mould, or in individual Savarin moulds or even small pudding moulds. Frying heat is needed to prepare the fruit garnish and flambé it, either a large spirit burner or a hotplate.

Savarin or Baba mixture

Cooking Time 15–20 mins. for small ones and 30–40 mins. for a large one.
Temperature 425° (220°C) for small ones, 400° (200°C) for large ones.
Quantities for 4–6 small moulds or one 7–8 in. (18–20 cm.) Savarin mould. Grease the moulds.

4 oz. plain flour (¾ c. or 125 g.)   5 Tbs. milk
½ oz. yeast (15 g.)   1 Tbs. sugar

Sift the flour into a basin and make a well in the centre. Heat the milk to lukewarm. Blend the yeast with the milk and pour the mixture into the flour. Sprinkle in the sugar and leave in a warm place until the yeast is frothy.

2 eggs   2 oz. butter (50 g.), almost melted

Beat the eggs and add to the flour together with the melted butter. Beat thoroughly for about five minutes, by hand or on slow speed with an electric mixer. It should thicken a bit and give a smooth batter. Pour it into the prepared moulds, half filling them. If small moulds are used stand them on a baking tray. Put moulds in a large polythene bag and leave in a warm place to rise almost to the tops, about 1 hr. Remove the polythene and bake the moulds until they feel springy on top. Turn out on a serving dish.

4 oz. sugar (½ c. or 125 g.)   4 Tbs. water   2–4 Tbs. rum

Boil the sugar and water together until it looks syrupy, about 5 mins. Add the rum and spoon carefully over the Savarin allowing it to soak in well. Keep the Savarin warm.

To Flambé and serve

8 oz. diced fruit (125 g.), fresh or canned

Drain canned fruit very thoroughly and prepare fruit as for a salad.

1 oz. butter (25 g.)   2 oz. caster sugar (4 Tbs.)

Heat the butter in a frying pan, add the sugar and cook gently, without stirring, until it turns a pale caramel colour. Add the fruit and heat it, basting with the sauce.

About 3 Tbs. rum, brandy or liqueur
2 Tbs. orange or lemon juice (use lemon for sweet canned fruits)

Add the spirit to the fruit, ignite. When it has burnt out add the fruit juice. Put the fruit in the centre of the Savarin and serve.

Accompaniments
Serve thin cream or whipped cream.

SWEET OMELET FLAMBÉ

This requires frying temperature, so use either a large spirit burner or a hotplate.

Quantities for 2.

4 eggs   1 tsp. grated lemon rind   2 tsp. double cream

Beat these together very thoroughly.

½ oz. butter (15 g.)

Melt the butter in a 7–8 in. (18–20 cm.) frying pan and when it is just beginning to colour, add the egg mixture. As it cooks, lift the edges to let uncooked mixture run below. When it is almost cooked, leave to brown underneath. Roll up and tip onto a hot metal serving dish.

Caster sugar   2–3 Tbs. warm rum or brandy, or a liqueur

Sprinkle the omelet with sugar, pour the warm spirit over it and ignite. Serve.

Alternative

Make individual omelets in a smaller pan or, for four people, make double the recipe in a 10 in. pan (25 cm.)

10 Quick Dishes for Frypan and Hotplate

These are all recipes which should be cooked at the last minute if they are to be at their best. They are suitable for side table cooking provided the table is equipped with either a hotplate, an electric frypan or a large spirit burner and trivet. You also need a food warmer on which to have the plates and any hot accompaniments.

For other suitable recipes for this type of cooking, see the following (those in the flambé section can be cooked without the flambé if you prefer that):

STEAK DIANE

For hotplate or frypan.

Cooking Time 5 mins.   *Quantities* for 4:

4 *portions fillet steak cut* ¼ *in. thick* (½ *cm.*)

1 *oz. butter* (25 *g.*)   2 *Tbs. oil*

Heat the frypan at 380° (190°C). Add the butter and oil and when the butter melts fry the steaks for 1–2 mins. each side. Remove and put them to keep hot. Turn the heat down to 240° (115° C).

2 *Tbs. Worcester sauce*   1 *Tbs. lemon juice*

Add to the pan, stir well and heat.

1 *Tbs. grated onion, or use finely-minced*
2 *tsp. chopped parsley*

Add to the pan and simmer for a minute. Pour over the steaks and serve.

Accompaniments
Potatoes or fresh rolls; a salad, see pages 183–7.

STEAK FRIED WITH VERY LITTLE FAT

Better in the frypan.

Have the steak cut in ¼ in. thick slices (½ cm.). Heat the frypan to 400° (200°C). When it is up to temperature add a little oil and tilt the pan to make a very thin film of oil on the surface. Pour off any surplus. Add the meat and cook quickly for 2–3 mins. each side. Serve it with your favourite accompaniments or turn it into a fried steak fondue, see page 40, or flambé it, see page 53

You will find there is quite a bit of sediment in the pan, don't waste this, swill out the pan with wine, stock or lemon juice, stirring with a wooden spoon to loosen the sediment. Pour the liquid over the steak as a sauce.

BEEF STROGONOFF

For hotplate or frypan.

Cooking Time 10–15 mins.   *Quantities* for 4.

1 *lb. thinly-sliced rump, sirloin or fillet steak* (½ *kg.*)

Beat the steak to flatten it. Cut it in strips about 2 in. (5 cm.) long and ¼ in. (½ cm.) wide.

1 medium-sized onion   6 oz. button mushrooms (175 g.)
Skin the onion and slice it very finely. Wash, dry and slice the mushrooms.

2 oz. butter (50 g.)

Heat the frypan at 320° (160°C.) and when it is up to temperature put in half the butter. When it has melted add the onions and fry them until they are lightly browned, stirring frequently. Add the mushrooms and fry for a few minutes. Remove onions and mushrooms and keep hot. Add the remaining butter and when it is melted add the beef and fry it for 3–4 mins., stirring frequently. Put back the onions and mushrooms and mix.

½ pt. sour or cultured cream (1 c. or 250 ml.)   Salt and pepper
Add the cream and season well. Cook for 1 min. Serve at once.

Accompaniments
Rice or buttered noodles; green salad.

HAM IN MADEIRA SAUCE
For the frypan.
Cooking Time 5–10 mins. provided the sauce has been made in advance.
Quantities for 4.

¾–1 lb. cooked sliced ham or boiled bacon (375–500 g.)
1 pt. Madeira sauce (2 c. or ½ l.) page 175

As all the ingredients for this are prepared in advance all you have to do is heat the sauce in the frypan at about 260° (130°C) until it is bubbling gently. Add the ham or bacon, turning and basting to coat it with the sauce. Allow to simmer for 5 mins. Then turn the heat down to 'warm' and leave until you are ready to serve it; but don't keep a long time.

Accompaniments
Buttered noodles; braised celery; green beans; broad beans; cooked chicory; leaf spinach; broad bean purée; pease pudding; rolls or bread and a salad.

TONGUE IN ESPAGNOLE OR MADEIRA SAUCE
Treat slices of boiled ox or calf's tongue in the same way as the ham in the above recipe. For Espagnole sauce, see page 175. This is a

good way of serving freshly-cooked tongue while it is hot, leaving the remainder to be served cold.

FRIED GAMMON IN SWEET MUSTARD SAUCE

Cooking Time 10–15 mins.   *Quantities* for 4.

4 portions of gammon about ¼–½ in. (½–1 cm.) thick
Lard or other fat

Remove any rind from the gammon and nick the fat at intervals to make the pieces stay flat during cooking. Heat the frypan to 340° (170°C) and when it is up to temperature add enough fat to make a thin film on the surface. Add the gammon and cook for 5–10 mins. or until done, turning two or three times during cooking as this helps to keep the pieces flat. Remove and keep hot. Turn the heat down to 260° (130°C).

2 Tbs. French mustard   1 oz. brown sugar (2 Tbs. or 50 g.)
1 tsp. paprika pepper
¼ pt. water, stock, cider or wine (½ c. or 150 ml.)

Mix these together and add them to the fat in the pan, pouring off some fat first if there seems to be rather a lot. Cook and stir for a few minutes. Return the gammon, cover the pan and heat for another 5 mins. Turn down to 'warm' until ready to serve.

Accompaniments
Boiled potatoes, rice or noodles and a salad.

LIVER AND BACON WITH RED WINE

For hotplate or frypan.

Cooking Time about 10 mins.   *Quantities* for 4.

¾–1 lb. calf's, lamb's or pig's liver (375–500 g.)
4–8 rashers streaky bacon

Ask the butcher to slice the liver very thinly or buy it in a piece and slice it yourself. If you have a supply of liver in the freezer you will find it very easy to slice it thinly when it is partially thawed. It can be cooked without complete thawing and is more juicy this way.

Remove rinds from the bacon.

Lard or oil

Heat the frypan at 340° (170°C), add just enough lard or oil to make a film on the surface of the pan. Add the bacon and fry until done

106

to your taste. Remove and keep hot. Turn up the heat to 360° (180°C), add the liver and cook quickly on both sides until browned. Avoid over-cooking as this makes it hard and tough. Remove the liver and keep hot.

$\frac{1}{4}$–$\frac{1}{2}$ *pt. red wine or a mixture of wine, stock and lemon juice ($\frac{1}{2}$–1 c. or 150–250 ml.)*

Turn down the heat to about 260° (130°C), add the liquid using enough to make the amount of gravy you like. Stir and boil to dissolve all the sediment. Season to taste, return the liver, make sure it is hot and then turn the control to 'warm' to keep hot until required.

Accompaniments
Sauté or boiled potatoes and a salad such as mixed green salad, page 185, or brussels sprouts and orange salad, page 183.

LIVER WITH ORANGE SAUCE

For hotplate or frypan.
Cooking Time about 5 mins.   *Quantities* for 2-3.

8 oz. very thinly sliced calf's or lamb's liver (250 g.)
1 oz. flour (3 Tbs.)   *1 tsp. salt*   *$\frac{1}{2}$ tsp. pepper*
$\frac{1}{2}$ tsp. dry mustard

Mix the flour and seasonings and coat the liver by shaking together in a paper bag or on a piece of clean paper.

1 oz. butter (25 g.)

Heat the frypan at 360° (180°C) and then add the butter. When it melts fry the liver quickly until brown on both sides. Remove and keep hot. Turn the frypan thermostat down to 260° (130°C).

1 oz. butter (25 g.)   *1 Tbs. onion juice*   *1 Tbs. chopped parsley*
4 Tbs. orange juice   *Grated rind of 1 orange*   *4 Tbs. red wine*

Add to the pan and stir and cook for 2–3 mins. Return the liver and make sure it is heated before serving.

Accompaniments
Potatoes or rice and a salad to follow, see pages 183–7.

LIVER VENEZIANA

For hotplate or frypan.
Cooking Time about 10 mins.   *Quantities* for 4–6.

1 lb. calf's or lamb's liver cut in very thin slices (½ kg.)

Wash and dry the liver and remove any stringy bits. Cut the thin slices in pieces about 1 in. square (2½ cm.).

4 medium-sized onions

Skin and slice very finely. This is most important.

4 Tbs. olive oil

Heat the frypan at 360° (180°C), add the oil, and fry the onions until brown. Add the pieces of liver and cook for 2 mins., stirring and tossing.

Salt and pepper
6 large sage leaves chopped finely, or more to taste
1 Tbs. chopped parsley.

Add and cook for ½ min. longer.

3–4 Tbs. red wine or stock

Add to the pan and stir to dissolve the sediment. Serve at once.

Accompaniments
Boiled or sauté potatoes followed by a salad, see pages 183–7.

LOBSTER NEWBURG

Suitable for hotplate or frypan.

Cooking Time 20 mins.   *Quantities* for 4.

2–4 cooked lobster tails, depending on the size

Remove the shell and carefully cut the meat into slices.

2 oz. butter (50 g.)

Heat the butter in a frying pan 300° (150°C) and fry the pieces of lobster gently to absorb the butter.

Madeira or sherry

Put in enough of the wine to cover the lobster and then boil until it has almost disappeared.

2 egg yolks   ½ pt. double cream (1 c. or 250 ml.)

Break up the egg yolks and gradually mix in the cream. Remove the pan from the heat, add the cream, and stir very gently, boiling until the sauce thickens. Serve hot.

Accompaniments
Buttered toast or boiled rice.

MEAT RISSOLES

The frypan is specially good for this kind of cooking because it is possible to cook the rissoles satisfactorily with very little fat or oil and thus avoid the greasiness which often spoils such a dish.

Cooking Time 10–15 mins.   *Quantities* for 4 rissoles.

8 oz. finely-minced cold, cooked meat (250 g.)
4 oz. mashed potato (125 g.)   1 very small onion, finely chopped
Salt and pepper   Grated nutmeg or ground mace
1 egg, beaten

Mix all the ingredients together thoroughly. If no fresh-mashed potato is available use an equivalent amount of made-up mashed potato powder (about 1 oz. (25 g.) powder). Should the rissole mixture seem a little dry, add wine or ketchup to moisten enough to bind. Turn the mixture onto a floured board and divide into four pieces. Shape each into a large round flat cake.

Oil

Heat the frypan at about 360° (185°C) and when it is up to temperature add a very little oil and tilt the pan to coat it with a film of oil. Add the rissoles and fry brown on both sides.

Accompaniments
Espagnole sauce, page 175; green salad, page 185.

11 Frypan Cooking in the Kitchen

The special features of the frypan make it ideal for cooking certain types of foods. It is excellent for preparing meat sautés where the meat is first fried, cooking continues slowly with the lid on the pan, and then a sauce is made in the pan or added to the juices in the pan. This cooking can be done on the side table but most people prefer to do it in the kitchen and then plug the frypan in at the side table to keep the sauté hot for serving.

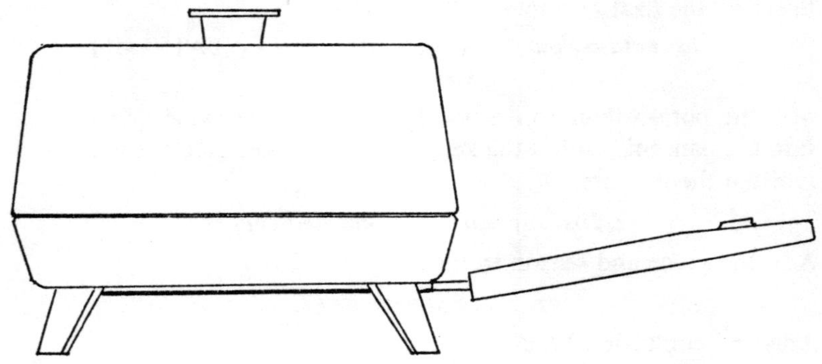

7. Electric frypan. White metal.

There are very many recipes for this classical type of cooking and I have included some of my favourites, together with recipes for other dishes which require a similar treatment.

I also find the frypan a great convenience for all the things one ideally wants to cook in a single layer and therefore needs a large pan for, things like poaching fruit for compotes, see page 123, cooking large flat fish like plaice or sole, see page 120, and marinading small whole fish, see page 120.

As with all special equipment start by reading the manufacturer's instruction booklet carefully and follow it until you see what the apparatus can do; then try other things. The recipes I have given here suggest times and temperatures. These are meant as a guide; your frypan may be different and there may be some adjustment needed.

For serving this type of food it is convenient to have a food warmer on the side table to take plates and hot accompaniments.

SAUTÉ OF CHICKEN WITH MUSHROOMS AND WALNUTS

Cooking Time about ½ hr.   *Quantities* for 4.

1 onion, finely chopped   1 green pepper, chopped   Oil

Heat the frypan at about 320° (160°C). When it is up to temperature add just enough oil to put a film on the surface. Add the onion and peppers and cook for a few minutes.

4 oz. sliced mushrooms (125 g.)
¾–1 lb. diced cooked chicken (375–500 g.)

Add mushrooms and chicken to the pan, mix and cook for 10 mins., lowering the heat to about 260° (130°C).

1 Tbs. potato flour   ¼ pt. white wine (½ c. or 150 ml.)
Chicken stock

Mix the potato flour to a smooth paste with the wine and pour it into the pan. Stir until it thickens, adding chicken stock as needed to moisten the mixture.

2 Tbs. soy sauce   Salt and pepper

Add the sauce and season to taste.

3 oz. chopped walnuts (75 g.)

Add and cook for 10 mins.

Accompaniments
Boiled rice or noodles and a green salad.

SAUTÉ OF CHICKEN WITH RED WINE

Cooking Time about 45 mins.   *Quantities* for 4.

4 portions of frying chicken   Seasoned flour

Wash and dry the chicken and coat the pieces with the flour.

1 Tbs. olive oil   ½ oz. butter (15 g.)

Heat the pan at 380° (190°C). When it is up to temperature add the

112

butter and oil and when the butter has melted fry the chicken pieces until they are well browned.

¼ *pt. red wine (½ c. or 150 ml.)*	1 *Tbs. finely chopped onion*
2 *oz. sliced mushrooms (50 g.)*	1 *Tbs. chopped green pepper*
Salt and pepper 2 *tomatoes, sliced*	1 *rasher bacon, chopped*

Add to the chicken in the pan and bring to the boil. Turn down the heat to about 260° (130°C), cover the pan and cook for a further 30 mins. or until the pieces of chicken are tender. If it seems necessary, add some more wine or some stock to the pan during cooking but there should not be a lot of liquid.

Accompaniments
Buttered noodles with spinach or green beans or a salad to follow, see pages 183–7.

SAUTÉ OF CHICKEN WITH TARRAGON SAUCE
Cooking Time about 45 mins.   *Quantities* for 4.
Begin by making the sauce in a small pan, to be kept hot.

½ *oz. fat* (15 g.)   1 *small onion*   1 *rasher bacon*

Remove the rind and chop the bacon. Skin and chop the onion finely. Heat the fat and fry bacon and onion until just beginning to brown.

1 *Tbs. flour*

Add and mix and cook until just beginning to brown.

½ *pt. chicken stock* (1 c. or 250 ml.)   2 *tsp. tomato paste*
Salt and pepper

Add to the pan and stir until boiling. Put to simmer while the chicken is cooked.

4 *portions frying chicken (breast or leg are the easiest to handle)*
1 *oz. butter* (25 g.)

Heat the frypan at 380° (190°C). Add the butter and let it melt, then add the chicken and fry until golden brown on both sides. Turn the heat down to 260° (130°C), put on the lid and cook until the chicken is tender, about 30 mins.

2 *Tbs. chopped fresh tarragon*   ¼ *pt. white wine (½ c. or 150 ml.)*

Remove the chicken and put to keep hot. Add the tarragon to the sauce and continue to keep hot. The reason for not adding this earlier is to preserve its fresh flavour. Add the wine to the frypan and stir until boiling, turning the heat up as necessary. Boil until reduced by half. Add the sauce and mix well. Return the pieces of chicken and turn them over in the sauce to coat them. Cook until they are well heated and then turn the control to 'warm' until required for service.

Accompaniments
Boiled or mashed potatoes; buttered noodles; green beans; mixed green salad, page 185.

SAUTÉ OF LAMB WITH CINNAMON AND SOUR CREAM
Cooking Time 40–50 mins.   *Quantities* for 4.

2 medium-sized onions   1 oz. butter (25 g.)
2 Tbs. olive oil

Skin the onions and chop them finely. Heat the frypan at 380° (190°C) and when it is hot add the butter and oil. When the butter has melted fry the onion until it just begins to brown.

1–1½ lb. lean boneless leg of lamb (½–¾ kg.)
½ tsp. ground cinnamon

Cut the meat in 1 in. cubes (2½ cm.) and sprinkle it with the cinnamon. Add to the onion and mix. Turn down the heat to 260° (130°C), cover and continue to cook until the meat is tender, about 30 mins.

½ pt. sour or cultured cream (1 c. or 250 ml.)   Salt and pepper

Add to the meat and turn up the heat to make it boil. Stir well and simmer for a few minutes. Season to taste and turn down the heat to 'warm' until ready to serve.

Accompaniments
Boiled potatoes; rice; buttered noodles; green beans or peas; spinach; mixed green salad, page 185.

SAUTÉ OF LAMB WITH PAPRIKA
Cooking Time 40–50 mins.   *Quantities* for 4.

2 medium-sized onions   1 oz. butter (25 g.)   2 Tbs. olive oil

Skin the onion and chop it finely. Heat the frypan to 380° (190°C) and when it is up to temperature, add the oil and butter. When the latter is melted, add the onion and fry until it is just beginning to brown.

2 tsp. paprika pepper

Sprinkle over the onion and cook for a few seconds longer.

1–1½ lb. lean, boneless lamb (leg) (500–750 g.)
Seasoned flour

Cut the lamb in pieces about 1 in. cubed (2½ cm.) and roll it in seasoned flour to coat well. Add to the pan, stir to coat with the onion mixture, turn down the heat to 260° (130°C), cover, and continue cooking until the meat is tender.

Sherry or wine

Add sufficient to make a little gravy for the meat. If you like a lot, add some stock as well and then thicken it with a little blended potato flour. When the liquid boils turn the heat down to 'warm' until ready to serve.

Accompaniments
Buttered noodles, sauté potatoes, green beans or peas or salad, see pages 183-7.

FRIED PORK AND GREEN PEPPERS

Cooking Time about 20 mins.   *Quantities* for 4–6.

1½ lb. fillet of pork (750 g.)

Cut the meat in thin strips 1½ in. long (3½ cm.) and about ¼ in. thick (½ cm.).

2 green peppers   2 cloves garlic
3 spring onions or 1 shallot

Remove core and seeds of the pepper and dice the rest. Finely chop the onion and mince or crush the garlic.

1 Tbs. flour   2 Tbs. soy sauce   1 Tbs. brown sugar

Mix to a paste with a little cold water.

1 Tbs. lard

Heat the frypan to about 340° (170°C) and add the lard, tilting the pan to coat the surface evenly. Fry the onions and garlic for a minute. Add the diced pepper and fry at 300° (150°C.) for 5 mins. Add the pork and fry, stirring and turning, until it changes colour. Add the soy sauce mixture together with enough stock or water to moisten the meat. Stir until it thickens and simmer for a few minutes. Test a piece of pork to make sure it is cooked through.

Rice or noodles and a green vegetable or salad, see pages 183–7.

SAUTÉ OF PORK CHOPS IN CIDER SAUCE

Cooking Time 30 mins. for the sauce, 15–20 mins. for the chops.
Quantities for 4.

1 *oz. lard or butter* (25 *g.*)   1 *large onion, chopped*

Melt the fat in a saucepan and fry the onion until it is almost cooked but not brown.

1 *Tbs. flour*

Add and mix well. Cook until it turns yellow.

½ *pt. stock or canned consommé* (1 *c. or* 250 *ml.*)
¼ *pt. cider* (½ *c. or* 150 *ml.*)   ½ *tsp. salt*
Pinch of pepper

Add and stir until it boils. Simmer, uncovered, for about 30 mins. This sauce may be made in advance and allowed to become cold.

4 *pork chops or cutlets*   *Lard or oil*

Heat the frypan to 360° (180°C) and when hot add a little lard or oil to make a thin coating on the pan. Add the meat and brown on both sides. Turn down the heat to 260° (130°C), cover and finish the cooking. Lift out the meat and keep hot. Add the sauce to the pan together with

1 *tsp. French mustard*   4 *Tbs. chopped gherkins*

Turn up the heat until it boils and stir to incorporate any sediment in the pan. Return the meat, re-heat, and turn the thermostat to 'warm' to keep until required for service.

Accompaniments
Mashed potatoes, or noodles, and spinach, carrots or green beans.

SAUTÉ OF PORK FILLET

Cooking Time 20–30 mins.   *Quantities for* 4.

1 *lb. pork fillet* (½ *kg.*)   ½ *oz. lard* (15 *g.*)

Cut the fillet into pieces about ¾ in. (2 cm.) thick. Heat the frypan at 360° (180°C) and then add the lard. Tilt the pan to coat the surface evenly. Add the slices of pork fillet and fry until brown on both sides and cooked through. Remove and keep hot.

1 small onion, chopped

Add more lard if necessary and fry the onion until almost tender.

6 sage leaves, finely chopped
½ pt. dry cider (1 c. or 250 ml.)
1 Tbs. concentrated tomato pureé
Salt and pepper

Add to the onions and stir and cook until the sauce has thickened a little. Return the pork, re-heat, turn to 'warm' and leave until ready to serve.

Accompaniments
Boiled rice or noodles with green peas or beans; or boiled potatoes and a salad, see pages 183–7.

SAUTÉ OF VEAL CHOPS OR CUTLETS WITH MUSHROOMS

Cooking Time 20–30 mins., depending on the size.
Quantities for 4.

4 veal chops or 8 cutlets   1 oz. butter (25 g.)
2 Tbs. olive oil

Heat the frypan at 360° (180°C) and when it is up to temperature add the butter and oil. When the butter is foaming add the meat and brown on both sides. Reduce the heat to 300° (150°C), cover the pan and cook slowly for the rest of the time, 15–20 mins. in all.

8 oz. sliced mushrooms (250 g.)

When the meat is half cooked add the mushrooms. Stir occasionally. Lift out the meat and keep hot.

¼ pt. sherry (½ c. or 150 ml.)
¼ pt. double cream (½ c. or 150 ml.)
Salt and pepper

Add the sherry and bring to the boil, stirring all the time. Add the cream and boil until the sauce thickens a little. Season to taste. Return the meat to the sauce, re-heat and turn the control to 'warm' until ready to serve the meat.

Accompaniments
Boiled potatoes or buttered noodles: spinach, green beans, peas or carrots.

SAUTÉ OF VEAL ESCALOPES

Cooking Time 10–15 mins.   *Quantities* for 4.

> 4 *thin escalopes*   1 *oz. butter* (25 g.)

Heat the frypan at 320° (160° C) and when it is up to temperature add the butter. When the butter is melted fry the veal quickly until brown on both sides. Remove and keep hot.

> 2 *Tbs. chopped onion*

Add to the pan and cook until almost tender.

> 3 *oz. sliced mushrooms* (75 g.)

Add and cook a few minutes longer.

> 5 *Tbs. white wine*   5 *Tbs. canned beef consommé or good stock*

Add to the vegetables and bring to the boil. Then turn the heat down to about 260° (130°C).

> ¼ *pt. double cream* (½ *c. or* 150 *ml.*)   *Salt and pepper*

Add the cream slowly and, when mixed in, season to taste and return the meat. Leave just long enough to heat, then turn down to 'warm' until required but do not leave too long.

> *Chopped parsley*

Sprinkle over the meat before serving.

Accompaniments
Boiled potatoes or noodles; spinach or green beans or salad, see pages 183–7.

VEAL CHOPS À LA HONGROISE

Cooking Time about 30 mins.   *Quantities* for 4.

> 4 *good-sized veal chops or 8 cutlets*
> *Salt   Paprika pepper*

Sprinkle the meat with salt and plenty of paprika pepper, rubbing it in.

> 1 *oz. butter* (25 g.)

Heat the frypan at 380° (190°C), and when it is hot add the butter. When it melts add the veal and fry it until brown on both sides.

> 2 *Tbs. finely chopped onion*

Sprinkle into the pan, turn down the heat to 260° (130°C), cover the pan and cook until the meat is cooked through, about 15–20 mins.

$\frac{1}{4}$ *pt. white wine ($\frac{1}{2}$ c. or 150 ml.)*
$\frac{1}{2}$ *pt. double cream or sour or cultured cream (1 c. or 250 ml.)*

Remove the meat from the pan and keep it hot. Add the wine to the pan, turn up the heat to make it boil rapidly and stir to incorporate the sediment in the pan. Boil for a minute or so to reduce it a little and then add the cream. Continue boiling until the sauce thickens a little. Return the meat, make sure it is hot and then turn the control down to 'warm' until ready to serve.

Accompaniments
Buttered noodles; saffron rice, page 192; mixed green salad, page 185; chicory salad, page 184.

BACON RASHERS WITH CIDER

These are like very good boiled bacon, without having to cook a whole joint, quick and economical.

Cooking Time 30 mins.   *Quantities* for 4.

4 *thick lean bacon rashers*
$\frac{1}{4}$ *pt. dry cider ($\frac{1}{2}$ c. or 150 ml.)*

Remove the rinds from the rashers and put them in a shallow dish, pour over the cider, cover and store in the refrigerator for a couple of hours, turning once. Transfer to the frypan and heat until boiling, then reduce the heat to about 220° (110°C) and cook gently, with the lid on for $\frac{1}{2}$ hr.

Fresh chopped herbs

Sprinkle over the meat and serve with the liquid as a sauce.

Accompaniments
Boiled potatoes, and root vegetables or spinach.

FRANKFURTERS WITH SAUERKRAUT

Cooking Time 20–30 mins.   *Quantities* for 4–5.

1 *small onion*   2 *Tbs. oil*

Skin and chop the onion. Heat the frypan to 380° (190°C), add the oil and fry the onion until it begins to brown.

1 *lb. sauerkraut ($\frac{1}{2}$ kg.)*   1 *lb. frankfurters ($\frac{1}{2}$ kg.)*
1 *lb. apples ($\frac{1}{2}$ kg.)*

Rinse the sauerkraut under the cold tap and drain for a few minutes.

Cut the frankfurters in 1 in. pieces (2 cm.). Peel and slice the apples. Add all three to the frypan.

¼ pt. white wine or stock (½ c. or 150 ml.)   *Pepper*

Add to the pan. When the mixture is boiling turn down the heat to stewing temperature, cover and cook until the apples are just tender. Serve hot.

Accompaniments
Boiled potatoes.

MARINADED HERRINGS OR OTHER SMALL FISH

To cook in advance and serve cold as hors d'oeuvre or as a main course with salad.

Cooking Time 25–30 mins.   *Quantities* for 6.

6 fresh herrings or small mackerel, or other small fish

After they have been cleaned and scaled the fish may be left whole, simply removing heads and tails. Alternatively, remove heads, bone the fish and then fold back into shape.

1 *small onion*   1 *small carrot*   1 *bay leaf*

Skin and chop the onion, scrape and slice the carrot; wash the bay leaf.

½ pt. white wine or dry cider (1 c. or 250 ml.)
¼ pt. white wine vinegar (½ c. or 125 ml.)
½ pt. water (1 c. or 250 ml.)
2 tsp. salt   Pinch of dried garlic

Put these in the frypan with the vegetables and bay leaf. Bring to the boil and turn down the heat to keep the liquid simmering, about 260° (130°C), for 15 mins. Put a lid on the pan to prevent evaporation, otherwise you will need to add some more water to have enough liquid in which to cook the fish. Add the fish and simmer for 10–20 mins., or until the fish is cooked, turn once during cooking. Put the fish in a flat dish and pour the liquid over it, cool, cover and store in the refrigerator. Serve with some of the strained liquid as a sauce.

SOLE OR PLAICE HOLLANDAISE

The electric frypan is ideal for poaching flat fish, whole or in fillets. Break the spine of the fish by folding it over in several places. This makes it much easier to eat 'on the bone'. Put the fish in the frypan, overlapping a little if necessary. Cover with water and add salt. Set the thermostat at 320° (160°C) until the water boils, then reduce the heat to 260° (130°C), cover and cook for 10 mins.

Chopped parsley   Boiled potatoes
Hollandaise sauce, see page 176

Drain the fish carefully and serve it garnished with parsley and serve the potatoes and sauce separately.

Alternative
Instead of the Hollandaise sauce serve melted butter and lemon wedges.

12 Sweets in the Frypan

The frypan is particularly useful for these, with its large surface enabling the fruit to be cooked in a single layer, and with its controlled temperature. Most compotes are served cold so this will not be side table cooking but, if you want to serve the fruit hot, plug in at the side table and turn to 'warm' to keep until required.

Compotes are made in the usual way, starting with a syrup, then poaching the fruit in that, lifting it out and reducing the syrup by fast boiling before finally pouring it over the fruit. If you are serving it hot you will want to omit this final reduction of syrup.

The following recipes are some suggestions to show the possibilities.

STEWED STUFFED APPLES

Cooking Time 20–30 mins.   *Quantities* for 4.

4 oz. sugar ($\frac{1}{2}$ c. or 125 g.)
$\frac{1}{2}$ pt. water or cider (1 c. or 250 ml.)

Put in the frypan and heat at 320° (160°C) until the sugar dissolves. Less sugar can be used if the apples are preferred rather tart or if dessert apples are used, e.g. small Coxes.

4–8 small apples

Peel and core the apples and put them in the hot syrup. When it boils again turn down the heat to 260° (130°C), cover with the lid and cook until tender, turning occasionally. Use a perforated spoon to lift the apples out into a shallow serving dish which is heat resistant.

*Red jam mixed with chopped nuts or a little dried fruit
and a pinch of ground cloves or cinnamon if liked*

Fill the centres of the apples with the jam mixture. Turn up the heat and boil the syrup remaining in the frypan until it begins to thicken a little. Pour it round the apples and allow them to become quite cold before serving with

Cream

DRIED APRICOT COMPOTE

Cooking Time about ½ hr.   *Quantities* for 4.

8 *oz. dried apricots* (250 *g.*)   4 *oz. seedless raisins* (½ *c. or* 125 *g.*)
1 *pt. water* (2 *c. or* ½ *l.*)   *Strip of lemon rind*

Put in the frypan and bring to the boil at about 320° (160°C). Put on the lid and turn down the heat to about 260° (130°C) until the apricots are tender, adding more water if necessary.

1 *large apple*

Peel and core and cut into eighths or thick slices. Put on top of the other fruit, cover the pan and cook until tender. Serve hot or cold.

Alternative
Add some diced canned pineapple to the compote before serving. In this case the pineapple juice could be used in place of some of the water in the compote.

FRESH APRICOT COMPOTE

Cooking Time 15–20 mins.   *Quantities* for 4.

1 *lb. apricots* (½ *kg.*)

Wash the fruit and cut in half, removing the stones. Crack these to extract some of the kernels and add to the fruit.

3 *oz. sugar* (75 *g.*)   ½ *pt. water* (1 *c. or* 250 *ml.*)

Put in the frypan and bring to the boil with the control at about 320° (160°C), stirring occasionally to dissolve the sugar. Add the prepared fruit and turn down the heat to 260° (130°C), cover and poach the fruit until it is just tender, turning once. Remove the fruit to a heat-proof dish, using a perforated spoon or ladle. Turn up the heat and boil the liquid hard until it is syrupy. Pour over the fruit and allow to become cold.

CHERRY COMPOTE

Cooking Time about 10 mins.   *Quantities* for 4.

1 *lb. cherries* (½ *kg.*)

Wash and drain the fruit. Remove stalks and any bad ones.

124

4 oz. sugar (½ c. or 125 g.)   ¼ pt. water (½ c. or 150 ml.)

Put in the frypan and bring to the boil at about 320° (160°C), stirring occasionally until the sugar is dissolved. Add the fruit and turn the heat down to 260° (130°C) to poach the fruit. Cover with the lid at this stage but turn the fruit over once during cooking. Lift the fruit out into a heat-proof dish using a perforated spoon or ladle. Turn the heat up to make the syrup boil fast and allow it to become syrupy. Pour over the fruit and allow to become cold.

Kirsch and cream (optional)

Add a little kirsch to the fruit before serving. Hand the cream separately.

PEACHES IN CIDER

Cooking Time 5–10 mins.   Quantities for 6.

2 oz. sugar (4 Tbs. or 50 g.)   ½ pt. cider (1 c. or 250 ml.)
¼ pt. water (½ c. or 150 ml.)

Put these in the frypan and bring to the boil at about 320° (160°C), stirring until the sugar dissolves. Turn down the heat and keep the syrup warm while the peaches are prepared.

6 ripe peaches

If these are the yellow kind and really ripe they can be skinned easily, otherwise put them in a bowl, cover with boiling water and leave for a couple of minutes. Pour off the hot water and cover with cold. The skins should then come off quite easily. Cut the peaches in half and remove the stones. Poach the fruit in the prepared syrup at about 260° (130°C) with the lid on and turning once during cooking. Put in a serving dish and pour the syrup over them. Leave to become cold.

3 Tbs. rum or maraschino (optional)

Add this just before serving.

PEAR CREAM

Cooking Time about 15 mins.   Quantities for 4.

4 firm, but not hard, pears

Peel, core and cut in large dice.

2 oz. brown sugar (4 Tbs. or 50 g.)
2 Tbs. granulated sugar
4 Tbs. unsweetened orange or pineapple juice

Put in the frypan with the diced pears and heat at 320° (160°C), stirring until the sugar dissolves. Cover and reduce the heat to 260° (130°C). Cook until the pears are tender. Turn up the heat again and cook until the mixture is syrupy, stirring occasionally until the pears look glazed and almost all the liquid gone. Remove from the pan, cool and chill in the refrigerator.

¼ pt. whipping cream (½ c. or 150 ml.)

Whip the cream and combine with the pear mixture just before serving. Serve in small glasses.

HONEY PEAR COMPOTE

Cooking Time ½–¾ hr. depending on the ripeness of the pears.
Quantities for 4.

4 oz. honey (125 g.)   ¼ pt. water (½ c. or 150 ml.)
1 piece of preserved ginger, chopped

Put in the frypan and begin to warm it while the pears are prepared. As each is ready turn it in the syrup to prevent discoloration.

4 firm dessert pears

Peel, halve, and core the pears and when all are ready turn up the heat to about 320° (160°C) until the syrup boils. Then turn down to about 260° (130°C) until the pears are just tender. Turn them occasionally during cooking and cook with the lid on the pan. Put in a serving dish and cover with the syrup. Allow to become cold and then chill.

Single cream (optional)

Hand the cream separately.

PEARS IN RED WINE SAUCE

Cooking Time about ½ hr.   Quantities for 4.

¼ pt. water (½ c. or 150 ml.)
¼ pt. red wine (½ c. or 150 ml.)
4 oz. sugar (½ c. or 125 g.)
Strip of lemon rind
Pinch of ground cinnamon

Put these in the frypan and bring to the boil at about 320° (160°C), stirring occasionally until the sugar dissolves.

4 ripe pears

Peel, halve, core and poach in the syrup at 260° (130°C) until just tender. Cover with a lid during cooking and turn the pears once. Remove pears to a heat-proof serving dish.

1 Tbs. potato flour

Blend this with a little cold water and use enough to thicken the liquid in the pan. Pour this over the pears.

Chopped roasted almonds   Whipped cream

Serve the pears when they are cold. Garnish with the nuts and cream.

PLUM COMPOTE

Cooking Time about 25 mins.   *Quantities* for 4.

4 oz. sugar (½ c. or 125 g.)   ½ pt. water

Put in the frypan and set the control at about 320° (160°C) until the sugar is dissolved and the syrup boils.

1 lb. plums (½ kg.)

Wash and remove stalks and any damaged parts. Add to the boiling syrup and when it boils again, cover the pan and turn the control down to 260° (130°C) and leave until they are just tender, turning once during cooking, about 20 mins.

Lift out the plums into a heat-resistant serving dish and turn up the controls to make the syrup boil fast to reduce and thicken it. Pour it over the plums and leave to become cold.

1 Tbs. kirsch

Sprinkle over the fruit when it is cold.

PRUNES IN CIDER

Cooking Time ½ hr.   *Quantities* for 4.

8 oz. plump prunes (250 g.)   ½ pt. water (1 c. or 250 ml.)

Soak these together overnight or until the prunes have swelled a little. Drain, putting the liquid in the frypan.

2 oz. sugar (4 Tbs. or 50 g.)

Add to the prune water in the frypan and bring to the boil at about

127

320° (160°C), stir until the sugar dissolves and then add the prunes. Turn the heat down to 260° (130°C).

4 pieces ginger preserved in syrup   5 Tbs. cider

Chop the ginger and add it to the prunes, with the cider. Cover the pan and cook until the prunes are tender. Allow to become cold before serving, with or without cream.

RHUBARB AND ORANGE COMPOTE

Cooking Time 20–30 mins.   *Quantities* for 4.

1 lb. rhubarb   2 oranges   3 oz. sugar (6 Tbs. or 75 g.)

Wash the rhubarb and trim off the ends. Cut it in 1 in. pieces (2½ cm.). Put in the frypan. Peel the oranges, slice and remove pips. Add to the rhubarb together with the sugar, sprinkled over. Cook at 300° (150°C) until the juice runs and begins to bubble. Turn down the heat to 260° (130°C) and continue cooking, covered, until the rhubarb is just tender. Serve hot or cold with or without

Cream

SPICED RHUBARB

Cooking Time 25–30 mins.   *Quantities* for 6–8.

2 lb. rhubarb (1 kg.)

Cut off the leafy tops and trim the root ends of the sticks. Wash well and cut in 1 in. (2½ cm.) pieces. Put in the frypan.

6–8 oz. sugar (175–250 g.)   4 cloves
1 tsp. ground cinnamon

Sprinkle these over the fruit, put on the lid with the vent closed and set the thermostat to about 300° (150°C). When liquid runs and begins to boil, turn down to about 260° (130°C) and cook until the rhubarb is just tender, but not mushy. Serve warm or chilled.

Using the Frypan as a Girdle (Griddle)

This is a useful cooking method which is difficult to manage on most conventional modern cookers. Using the frypan as a girdle enables you to have freshly-made scones and quick breads without using the oven and it gives results quite as good as the old-fashioned iron girdle of our grandmothers' kitchens.

You can cook these scones and quick breads on the side table and serve them hot.

For girdle cooking of toasted sandwiches, see page 158.

DROP SCONES OR SCOTCH PANCAKES

Cooking Time 3–4 mins. per batch.
Quantities for 12 large or 18 small scones.

2 *eggs*   1 *oz. sugar* (2 *Tbs.* or 25 *g.*)

Beat together in a mixing bowl until very thick and light.

4 *oz. self-raising flour* ($\frac{3}{4}$ *c.* or 125 *g.*) $\frac{1}{4}$ *tsp. salt*

Sift into the egg mixture and mix in.

$\frac{1}{2}$ *oz. melted butter or margarine* (1 *Tbs.* or 15 *g.*)
4–5 *Tbs. milk*

Add the melted fat and enough milk to make a thick batter which will pour slowly from the tip of a spoon. Don't beat this batter or the scones will be tough instead of light and soft. Heat the frypan at 380° (190°C) and when it is up to temperature grease it with a very little lard or oil. Drop the batter from the tip of a tablespoon or dessert spoon held upright, and putting several spoonfuls in at once as long as they are not close enough to run together. When bubbles begin to show on top turn the scones with a palette knife and cook the other side until brown. Put on a wire rack to cool a little. Then serve while still warm, with butter and jam, honey or syrup.

There is no need to re-grease the pan between batches.

GIRDLE SCONES

Useful to make to eat in place of bread in an emergency or to have fresh and hot for any tea-time.

Cooking Time 20–25 mins.   *Quantities* for 8 large scones.

8 *oz. self-raising flour* (1$\frac{1}{2}$ *c.* or 250 *g.*)
Pinch of salt   2 *oz. margarine* (50 *g.*)

Mix the flour and salt in a bowl and rub in the margarine.

1 *egg*   *Milk to mix, about* $\frac{1}{4}$ *pt.* ($\frac{1}{2}$ *c. or* 150 *ml.*)

Beat the egg and use it and the milk to mix to a very soft dough, form the dough into a ball and roll it out on a floured board to make a circle about $\frac{1}{2}$ in. (1 cm.) thick. Cut it into 8 triangles.

Heat the frypan at 360° (180°C) and when it is up to temperature grease the bottom lightly with a little lard. Cook the scones, turning when they are brown on one side and have risen. Use a palette knife or fish slice for turning them. Cook until the other side is browned and the scones cooked through. They are nicest served while still warm, with butter and jam or clotted cream and jam, or just with butter.

CHEESE GIRDLE SCONES

Add to the recipe above, after the margarine has been rubbed in,

2–3 oz. strongly-flavoured, finely-grated cheese (50–75 g.)

DATE GIRDLE SCONES

Add to the recipe for Girdle Scones, above,

3 oz. chopped dates (75 g.)

Add after the margarine has been rubbed in

1 Tbs. black treacle

Add with the egg and milk, using less milk than usual.

SWEET GIRDLE SCONES

Add to the recipe for Girdle Scones, above, after the margarine has been rubbed in,

2 Tbs. sugar

WHOLE WHEATMEAL GIRDLE SCONES

Make the recipe above for Girdle Scones, substituting 100 per cent whole wheatmeal self-raising flour for the white flour. These are very good eaten warm or cold, especially with honey for a sweet spread or with cheese.

WELSH GIRDLE CAKES

Cooking Time 10 mins.   *Quantities* for 18 cakes.

8 oz. self-raising flour (1½ c. or 250 g.)
½ tsp. salt   3 oz. butter or margarine (75 g.)

Sift flour and salt into a basin and rub in the fat.

3 oz. sugar (6 Tbs. or 75 g.)   3 oz. currants (½ c. or 75 g.)

Add to the flour and mix.

130

1 egg   Milk or water to mix

Beat the egg and use it, with enough milk or water to mix to a stiff dough like pastry. Roll out ¼in. thick (½ cm.) and cut in 2½ in. rounds (7 cm.). Heat the frypan at 360° (185°C), grease it and cook the cakes 5 mins. each side. Dredge with sugar and serve warm or cold, in place of cake.

You will probably need to cook these in two batches, but it won't hurt half the mixture to wait.

PAIN PERDU

Cooking Time a few mins.   *Quantities* for 4.

4 slices bread from a large loaf, cut about ½ in. thick (1 cm.)
¼ pt. milk (½ c. or 150 ml.)   1 Tbs. sugar   ½ tsp. vanilla

Trim crusts from the bread. Dissolve the sugar in the milk and add the vanilla. Dip the bread in this and drain.

1 egg   1 tsp. sugar

Beat together. Dip the bread in this.

1 oz. butter (25 g.)

Heat the frypan at 360° (180°C) and when it is up to temperature add the butter. When it foams fry the bread quickly until brown on both sides.

Vanilla sugar, sugar and cinnamon, or golden syrup, or honey

Serve the bread with one of these. The ideal is to serve the Pain Perdu as soon as cooked, but it will keep hot for a short while without spoiling,

13 Grills

Grills served in restaurants and snack bars have long been popular with the public, but it has often been difficult to produce good results with grills on domestic cookers. Now times are changing and grills improving. We now have better grills on cookers and very good portable or table-top grills of various designs. There has also been a big increase in the variety of grills for barbecue or outdoor grilling.

Grilled foods are only good if freshly cooked, as required; a side table grill enables you to achieve this without having to depart to the kitchen. The family can learn to cook their own to their particular tastes.

The fuel for table-top grills is most often electricity but they are also available using gas, bottled gas and charcoal, though the last two are usually designed for outdoor use and it is safer to restrict their use in this way. A charcoal grill can be fitted in a dining room with special ventilation and this then lessens the hazard from fumes given off.

When you buy an appliance make sure there is a good instruction booklet with it and that you understand the fundamentals. Read it carefully and keep it handy for reference. Make sure the apparatus is correctly and safely connected up, and that there are no trailing flexes or projecting handles in positions where they could cause accidents.

When grilling is done on a side table, or on the patio, or terrace, you also need a food warmer for plates and hot accompaniments.

As far as the actual cooking processes are concerned, grilling is just grilling whatever the design of the apparatus. The only thing likely to vary is the cooking time because some grills are hotter than others. With some if may not be possible to vary the heat, nor the distance you can place the food from the heat source to slow up the cooking when this is desirable; in these cases there are a few grills requiring gentle heat which it may be difficult to do to perfection.

In the recipes I have given guide-times, but if your instruction booklet says to use different times, follow these to begin with and then, if necessary, experiment to get the exact results you want.

In addition to the recipes here the following grills will be found in other parts of the book. Those in the flambé section can be served as plain grills if you prefer.

Grilled Steak served as a Fondue, page 40.

Barbecued Chicken Halves, page 54.

Grilled Lamb Chops with Lemon and Ginger Marinade, page 57.

Grilled Fillet of Pork, page 60.

Brochettes and Kebabs, pages 67–79.

Fruit Kebabs, pages 89–90.

Grilled and Toasted Sandwiches and Snacks, pages 151–165.

Grilled Vegetables, pages 188–9.

GRILLED BEEFSTEAK

Cooking Times	*Rare*	*Medium*	*Well-done*
½ in. thick (1 cm.)	7 mins.	9 mins.	11 mins.
1 in. thick (2½ cm.)	10 mins.	12 mins.	14 mins.

These times are only a guide and will vary with the type of grill you have. If there are no manufacturer's instructions use the above times to begin with and adjust them as necessary.

Quantities Allow 6–8 oz. per portion (175–250 g.).

Cuts to Use Fillet, rump or sirloin.

To Grill

Score the fat round a sirloin steak to keep the meat flat, taking the cuts right through to the beginning of the meat itself; alternatively, remove the fat. Brush the steaks with oil and pre-heat the grill. Cook the steak under a fierce heat for 1 min. each side, then reduce the heat slightly or move the meat further away from the grill and continue cooking, turning every 2 mins. Season with salt and pepper.

Accompaniments

Grilled tomatoes, page 189; grilled mushrooms, page 189; watercress; chip potatoes; baked jacket potatoes; maître d'hôtel butter, page 171; anchovy butter, page 170; garlic butter, page 171; grated fresh horseradish or horseradish sauce, page 177; fried onions;

134

mixed green salad, page 185; French or English mustard; Worcester-shire sauce.

GRILLED FROZEN STEAKS

Cooking Times	Rare	Medium	Well-done
½ in. thick (1 cm.)	9 mins.	11 mins.	13 mins.

(frozen steaks are not
usually thicker than this)

Brush the steaks with oil and put them 1–2 in. (2½–5 cm.) further from the heat than normal, until the meat is thawed. Put it closer to the heat for quick browning at the end.

GRILLED CHOPS AND CUTLETS

Cooking Times
Lamb cutlets   7–10 mins.
Lamb chops   10–20 mins. (according to the thickness)
Pork or Veal cutlets 10 mins.
Pork or Veal chops 20 mins.

Quantities Allow 1 chop or 2 cutlets per portion.

Cuts to use
Lamb—Loin chops or best end of neck cutlets
Pork —Loin chops or spare rib cutlets
Veal —Loin chops or neck cutlets

To Grill
Trim off surplus fat. With cutlets it is customary to trim the bones of fat and meat up to the thick meaty bit or 'eye'.

Brush the meat with oil and preheat the grill. Turn frequently during grilling under a moderate heat so that browning and cooking are finished together. It is a good idea to brush pork and veal with a basting sauce once or twice, see page 167.

Lamb should be cooked until it is just pink by the bone but other meats should be well done. If in doubt of the timing, cut one to see.

Accompaniments

Lamb
Maître d'hôtel butter, page 171; garlic butter, page 171; tarragon butter, page 172; mushroom sauce, page 178; onion sauce, page 179; fried potatoes; grilled potato and cheese balls, page 189; rice with

herbs, page 190; grilled aubergines, page 188; a salad from pages 183–7.

For those who like meat and fruit together put a slice of orange or pineapple on top of the meat when it is half-cooked, brush the fruit with oil and continue cooking.

Pork
Grilled tomatoes, page 189; grilled sweet peppers, page 189; grilled mushrooms, page 189; grilled apples and cheese, page 188; grilled bananas, page 188; apple sauce, page 172; red currant jelly; grilled halves of canned peaches; creamed potatoes or potato purée.

Veal
Espagnole sauce, page 175; anchovy butter, page 170; paprika butter, page 171; tarragon butter, page 172; saffron rice, page 192; creamed potatoes; mixed green salad, page 185; orange salad, page 186.

GRILLED FROZEN CHOPS AND CUTLETS

Cooking Times
Lamb cutlets   12–15 mins.
Lamb chops   15–20 mins.
Pork or Veal cutlets 20–25 mins.
Pork or Veal chops 30 mins.

Place the meat 1–2 in. (2½–5 cm.) further from the heat than is normal until the meat has thawed. Put it closer to the heat for quick browning at the end.

STEAK MIRABEAU

Cooking Time 8–10 mins.   *Quantities* for 4.

1 *oz. butter* (25 g.)   ½ *tsp. anchovy essence*

Soften the butter, without melting, and work in the anchovy essence, using a pestle and mortar if available. Form into a small pat and divide into four pieces. Put in the refrigerator until required.

8 *anchovy fillets*   *Stoned green olives*
Fresh tarragon leaves

Rinse the anchovy fillets in warm water and drain well. Wash and drain the tarragon leaves. Stone the olives if not already done.

136

4 small beefsteaks, fillet, rump or sirloin.   Olive oil

Brush the steaks with oil and grill them under a fierce heat, turning once to brown both sides. Cook until done to taste.

Put a pat of anchovy butter on top of each and decorate with the anchovy fillets and tarragon leaves.

Accompaniments
Boiled or sauté potatoes and a salad.

SPATCHCOCK GRILLED CHICKEN

Cooking Time ½–¾ hr.   *Quantities* Allow 1 poussin or small spring chicken per portion.

Salt and pepper   Lemon juice   Melted butter

Split the chicken in half down the backbone. Flatten the bird and secure in that position by passing a skewer through the legs. Sprinkle with salt and pepper and lemon juice. Set aside for ½ hr.

Grill, brushing during cooking with more butter. Cook under a high heat for 5 mins. each side or until brown, and then reduce the heat for the rest of the time.

Accompaniments
Fried or sauté potatoes; grilled tomatoes, page 189; grilled mushrooms, page 189; grilled aubergines, page 188; grilled sweet peppers, page 189; mixed salad, page 185; chicory and olive salad, page 184; orange and onion salad, page 187; grilled bananas, page 188.

GRILLED KIDNEYS (lamb's or pig's)

Cooking Time 5–10 mins.

They may be grilled whole with some of the layer of fat still left on to act as a basting liquid. Grill gently first one side and then the other until the fat has melted and beads of blood begin to appear on the surface of the kidney.

Alternatively remove the fat, skin the kidneys, and cut out the central hard core using a pair of kitchen scissors.

Grill them whole, or cut in halves almost through and opened out like a book. Grill each side until beads of blood begin to appear on the surface.

Accompaniments
Grilled bacon, chip potatoes and a salad; or serve them as part of a mixed grill.

GRILLED LAMB STEAKS

Cooking Time 25–30 mins.   *Quantities* for 4.

1–1½ lb. lean lamb steaks (½–¾ kg.)

The steaks should be cut from the top of the leg and should be 1–2 in. thick (2½–5 cm.). The lamb should be well hung or, if it is frozen lamb, keep it in the refrigerator for 2–3 days after thawing and before cooking. Grill the steaks under a medium heat, turning frequently. For the last few minutes of cooking brush several times with

Just-melted red currant jelly

Accompaniments

More red currant jelly; mint sauce, page 178; Cumberland sauce, page 174; sauté potatoes, page 190; rice with herbs, page 190; green peas or beans; grilled vegetables, pages 188–9.

GRILLED LIVER WITH PICKLED BEETROOT

Cooking Time 5–8 mins.   *Quantities* for 4.

*1 lb. calf's, lamb's or pig's liver (½ kg.) cut in ½ in. thick
slices (1 cm.)   Oil or a barbecue sauce, see page 167*

Remove any tubes and fibres from the liver. Wash it in cold water and dry on paper towels. Brush with oil or a basting sauce and grill quickly, turning once. As soon as beads of blood begin to appear on the surface of the liver it is cooked enough.

*4 medium pickled beetroot or 8 baby beets, diced
1 oz. butter (25 g.)   1 Tbs. capers*

While the liver is cooking heat the butter and warm the beetroot in it. Add the capers and keep warm.

Salt and pepper   Watercress or lettuce

When the liver is cooked, season it with salt and pepper and serve with the beetroot and a garnish of watercress or lettuce.

Accompaniments

Boiled potatoes tossed in melted butter and chopped parsley or chives. For those who like a sauce, serve Espagnole, page 175, or a savoury butter, page 170. Serve a salad to follow, see pages 183–7.

GRILLED MEATBURGERS

Cooking Time 15–20 mins.   *Quantities* for 4.

2 *Tbs. chopped onion   A little fat or oil*

Fry the onion until tender. Set aside to cool.

1 *lb. lean raw minced meat* ($\frac{1}{2}$ *kg.*) $\frac{1}{2}$ *c. fresh breadcrumbs* (150 *ml.*)
1 *tsp. salt* (*include some garlic or celery salt if liked*)
$\frac{1}{4}$ *tsp. freshly-ground pepper* $\frac{1}{4}$ *tsp. ground mace or nutmeg*
Chopped or dried herbs (*marjoram, basil, savory, thyme*) *to taste*
4–8 *Tbs. milk or water* (*include some red wine if liked*)

The meat can be beef or lamb or a mixture of beef, pork or veal. Minced bacon, liver, heart or kidney can be included as well as some sausage meat.

Put all in a bowl with the onion. Mix well using a wooden spoon, and working until the mixture is smooth, adding liquid as needed. The mixture should be moist without being difficult to handle. Turn out and shape with floured hands. Divide the mixture into eight equal portions and shape each into a cake about $\frac{1}{2}$ in. thick (1 cm.).

Heat the grill and grease the rack or grids. Grill the meatburgers under a fierce heat until browned, and then more slowly to finish cooking. Cut one to make sure it is done.

Accompaniments
Grilled tomatoes or mushrooms; fried or mashed potatoes; fried onions; tomato sauce or Espagnole sauce, page 175; green salad; green peas or beans; cauliflower with cheese sauce.

GRILLED SAUSAGES WITH BACON ROLLS AND APPLE RINGS

Cooking Time 20–30 mins.   *Quantities* for 4.

1–1$\frac{1}{2}$ *lb. pork sausages* ($\frac{1}{2}$–$\frac{3}{4}$ *kg.*)

Separate the sausages, put them on the grill rack and cook fairly slowly, turning frequently until they are well browned and cooked right through. Cut one open to be sure.

4–8 *thin rashers of streaky bacon   2 cooking apples*

Trim rinds from the bacon and roll it up. Secure with cocktail sticks or thread on a skewer.

Peel the apples, remove core with an apple corer and cut the apples in slices about $\frac{1}{2}$ in. (1 cm.) thick, brush with oil.

When the sausages are half cooked, put the bacon and apple beside them, turning frequently until the bacon is crisp and the apples tender.

If there isn't room for all this beside the sausages, the apples can be cooked underneath the rack, but in this case allow longer cooking time. Otherwise make apple sauce instead of grilling the apple.

Alternatives
Other fruit may be substituted for the apples, for example, peeled bananas, canned peach halves or pineapple rings.

BARBECUED STEAKS OR FILLETS OF FISH

Cooking Time 10–15 mins., depending on the thickness.
Quantities allow 1 steak or 6–8 oz. (175–250 g.) fillet per person.

Basting Sauce   Quantities for 4.

> 2 *Tbs. oil*   1–2 *tsp. lemon juice*   ¼ *tsp. salt*
> *Pinch of pepper*   1 *tsp. anchovy essence*

Mix these together and brush over the fish before cooking and during cooking. Heat the grill and cook the fish under a moderate heat until brown on one side and the flesh is showing opaque halfway through. Turn, brush the top with basting sauce and continue grilling until brown and cooked through.

Accompaniments
Done this way the fish is good just with lemon wedges, potatoes and a salad, or grilled tomatoes and mushrooms. If a sauce is preferred, serve Tartare, page 170, or one of the savoury butters, page 170, or egg sauce, page 175.

Alternative Flavourings for the Basting Sauce
Instead of the anchovy essence add one of the following:

> 1 *Tbs. finely chopped onion*   1 *tsp. prepared mustard*
> 1 *tsp. Worcester sauce*   1 *Tbs. ketchup*

GRILLED HERRINGS WITH MUSTARD BUTTER

Cooking Time 8–10 mins.   *Quantities* for 4.

> 4 *herrings*   *Seasoned flour*

Bone the herrings, open out flat and dip in the flour to coat them well.

140

2 oz. softened but not melted butter (50 g.)
2 tsp. dry mustard   2 tsp. lemon juice

Mix the butter and flavourings. Spread a little of the butter on each herring and grill the fish under a medium heat to brown on both sides. Serve with more of the butter on each herring.

Accompaniments
Boiled potatoes or bread and butter, and a salad, see pages 183–7.

GRILLED MACKEREL

Cooking Time 10–15 mins. according to size, longer for very large ones.

Quantities. Allow 1 fish per person.

Wash and clean the fish. Remove heads or leave on. With a small sharp knife, cut along the backbone to open the fish but not divide it completely in two. The object of this cut is to allow heat to penetrate to the thickest part of the fish and also to allow the backbone to be easily removed when the fish is served.

Salt and pepper   Melted butter (about 2 Tbs.)

Season the fish inside and out and brush with melted butter. Grill, turning once, and again brushing with melted butter

Half-melted maître d'hôtel butter, page 171, *or*
Mustard butter, page 171   *Lemon wedges*

When the fish is cooked, sprinkle it with the half-melted butter sauce and serve with lemon wedges.

Accompaniments
Boiled potatoes and a green salad, or tomato and cucumber salad.

Alternative
Instead of the melted butter sauce, serve separately, salsa verde sauce, page 179, or horseradish sauce, page 177.

GRILLED RED MULLET

Cooking Time 10–15 mins.   *Quantities* Allow 1 fish per person.

This fish is not usually cleaned, but is scaled and the gills pulled out. Wipe the fish with paper towels. With a small sharp knife cut gashes each side, fairly close together, to allow heat to penetrate during cooking.

Salt and pepper   Oil   Lemon juice
Slices of lemon   Parsley stalks

Season the fish and sprinkle with a little lemon juice and oil. Put a few slices of lemon and some parsley stalks underneath and on top of the fish, in a shallow dish. Leave to marinate for an hour, turning it occasionally. Grill, turning once, and serve with

Half-melted maître d'hôtel butter, page 171.

handed separately.

Accompaniments
Boiled potatoes and a salad, see pages 183–7.

SOLE OR PLAICE ST-GERMAIN

Cooking Time 10–15 mins.   *Quantities* Allow one fish per person.

Sole or plaice   Melted butter   Fine fresh breadcrumbs

Season the fish with salt and pepper and dip it in melted butter and then in breadcrumbs, patting the crumbs on firmly with a palette knife. Sprinkle with more melted butter (or oil), and grill slowly so that the crumbs become golden by the time the fish is cooked.

Accompaniments
Parisian potatoes cooked in clarified butter, page 189, Béarnaise sauce, page 172.

14 Spit-Roasting

I have included this short chapter on spit-roasting because there are a number of portable rôtisseries available and there is no reason why they shouldn't be used in the dining room if that is more convenient than the kitchen. They are, too, ideal for an outdoor meal on the patio, always provided that you have a suitable electric socket available. Some of the portable charcoal grills have a rôtisserie attachment which is mechanically operated and these are fine for all outdoor cooking.

The spit-roaster or rôtisserie can be used for cooking any good quality roasting meat which is a suitable shape for fixing on the rotating spit. Boned and rolled joints are the easiest to handle, but more difficult shapes can be satisfactorily spit-roasted provided care is taken in fixing them in position. Boned meat and poultry can be stuffed before cooking.

One of the advantages of spit-roasting is that the meat is self-basting, though very lean meats need some assistance. Lean joints can have a piece of fat tied round them (suet, caul fat, salt pork, bacon). The fat should be thin otherwise it will impede the normal browning of the joint and will have to be removed at the end of cooking to allow browning to take place. An alternative to the piece of fat is to baste a lean joint with oil or melted butter. Basting sauces (see pages 167–8) are used for extra flavour but some of them (those containing tomato and other ingredients which cause dark browning) should not be used until towards the end of the cooking time.

Cooking Times
These vary with the make of rôtisserie and it is advisable to follow the manufacturer's instructions. The following list is meant as a guide.

Joints—20–30 mins. per lb. ($\frac{1}{2}$ kg.).
Medium-sized broiler chickens—45–60 mins.

Small stuffed turkey—20 mins. per lb. ($\frac{1}{2}$ kg.).
Ducklings—15–20 mins. per lb. ($\frac{1}{2}$ kg.). Prick the skin well to allow
    fat to escape.
Pheasant—15–20 mins. per lb. ($\frac{1}{2}$ kg.).
Other small birds—$\frac{1}{2}$–$\frac{3}{4}$ hr. depending on the size.

Using the Spit-Roaster
As with all specialised apparatus it is advisable to follow the maker's
instructions when you are learning how to use it.

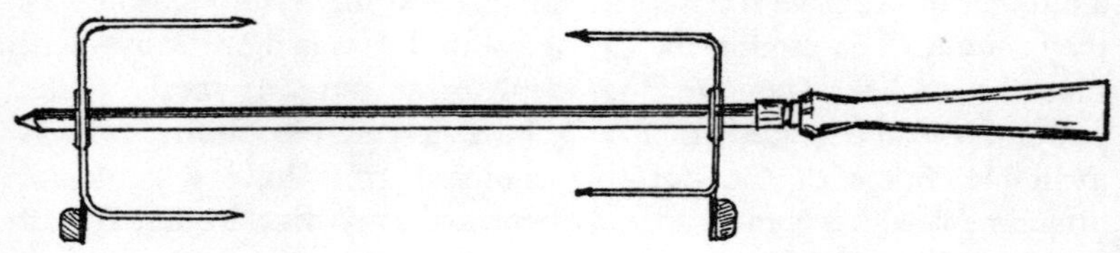

8. Spit for rotary grill. Central spigot is square in section;
prongs (for meat, etc.) are circular.

Before starting to cook the meat it is most important to see that it
is evenly placed on the spit and securely fastened there by the clips
provided. If the spit doesn't revolve easily and evenly, remove and re-
centre the piece of meat.

BROCHETTES AND KEBABS

Most modern spit-roasters have attachments for kebab skewers, and
this is the best way of cooking these delicious foods. Recipes will be
found on pages 67–79 and 89–90, but the flambé part of the recipe
can be omitted if you prefer it.

SPIT-ROASTED BACON JOINT WITH HONEY GLAZE

Cooking Time

Boiling for 15 mins. per lb. ($\frac{1}{2}$ kg.), then spit-roasting for 30–40 mins.,
depending on the size of the joint.

Cuts to Use

A boned and rolled piece is best, with a fair covering of outside fat,
gammon, forehock and prime collar being the best. Use a piece

144

weighing from 2–5 lb. (1–2 kg.). Allow 4–6 oz. per portion (125–175 g.).

Cooking

A preliminary boiling is needed but first, if the joint is a salty one, soak it in cold water to cover, for 2–3 hrs. or over-night. Drain, put in a pan and cover with fresh cold water. Bring to the boil and simmer for 15 mins. per lb. (½ kg.). Drain.

Cut off the rind using a fork to hold the hot meat. Score the fat in a diamond pattern, fasten the meat on the spit and secure it firmly. Make sure it is tied firmly in shape, adding more ties if necessary.

Glaze

1–2 *tsp. dry mustard*   1–2 *tsp. Worcester sauce*
2–4 *Tbs. clear honey or warmed thick honey*

Use the larger amounts for a joint of 3 lb. or more (1½ kg.). Mix the mustard to a paste with the sauce and then add the honey. Brush the meat all over with this and again during cooking.

Spit-Roasting

Put the joint on the spit-roaster and switch to high heat or adjust position of the rod to give maximum heat, according to the type of roaster being used. Cook at high heat for 10 mins., then lower the heat for the remaining time. Use the longer time of 30 mins. for the larger joints. Remove from the spit and leave to stand for 5 mins. or more before carving.

Accompaniments

For the sauce you can use more of the glazing sauce if you like sweet sauces with bacon, otherwise serve a sharp sauce such as mustard sauce, page 178, or ketchup and cream sauce, page 177, or for a milder flavour use Béchamel sauce, page 173, flavoured with herbs, or Cumberland sauce, page174 .

Serve potatoes and other vegetables or salad, according to taste.

SPIT-ROASTED BEEF

Cooking Time 20–30 mins. per lb. (½ kg.).

The time depends on the shape of the piece as well as on the weight and on whether it is preferred well done or rare in the middle. A piece thick in proportion to its length will take relatively longer per lb. to cook.

Cuts to Use
For best results use only the finest roasting cuts such as boned sirloin
or a large piece of rump steak. If you can be sure of getting really top-
quality boned rib roasts or topside these can be spit-roasted but it is
really safer to roast them in the oven.

Preparation
Make sure the meat is tied securely at about 1½ in. (3–4 cm.) intervals and in as even a shape as possible. Very lean meat will either
need basting with oil or an oil-based sauce, see page 167; or have a
piece of fat tied round it to act as a self-baster—but only a thin piece
of fat—*not* the chunk of fat some butchers tie round topside. If you
do have too much fat it will be troublesome with excess dripping and
the fat itself acts as an insulation and prevents the even penetration
of heat.

Cooking
Use a high heat until the meat is thoroughly browned all over and
then reduce the heat for the remainder of the cooking time. After
cooking put the meat in a warming cupboard or warm oven to stand
for about 10 mins. before carving; this makes carving easier.

Accompaniments
Serve the gravy which runs out of the meat during carving. In addition
offer horseradish sauce, bottled or see page 177; Cumberland sauce,
page 174; French or English mustard; plus potatoes cooked any way
and additional vegetables or a salad, see pages 183–7.

SPIT-ROASTED CHICKEN

Cooking Time 1 hr.　*Quantities* for 4.

4 *Tbs. oil*
1 *tsp. each of dried powdered thyme, tarragon and rosemary*

Infuse the herbs in the oil for an hour or longer.

2½ *lb. roasting chicken*　　*Salt and pepper*
1 *bay leaf or a sprig of rosemary*

Salt the inside and outside of the chicken and put the bay leaf or rosemary inside. Put the chicken on a platter and rub it all over with the
oil mixture, Leave to stand for an hour at room temperature or
several hours in the refrigerator.

To truss a chicken for the spit turn under the neck skin and skewer

146

it to the back with a cocktail stick. Fold the wings backwards in the usual way and secure them with a piece of string tied right round the top of the bird. Tie the legs and tail together. Run the spit through parallel to the backbone and fasten so that the weight is evenly distributed.

Cook at high heat until the skin is well browned and then reduce the heat to finish cooking.

SPIT-ROASTED LEG OF LAMB

Cooking Time 30 mins. per lb. ($\frac{1}{2}$ kg.).

> 2 *Tbs. Worcester sauce*　　2 *Tbs. tomato ketchup*
> 1 *tsp. anchovy essence*　　1 *Tbs. made mustard*
> $\frac{1}{2}$ *clove finely chopped or crushed garlic*

Mix these together and use to baste the meat several times during the last part of the cooking time. Some spit-roasters have a special holder for legs of lamb or other small legs but if yours has just the spit rod make sure it is threaded so that the weight is evenly distributed.

Cook at high heat until browned and then reduce the heat for the remainder of the cooking time.

SPIT-ROASTED SHOULDER OF LAMB

Cooking Time 30 mins. per lb. ($\frac{1}{2}$ kg.).

$\frac{1}{2}$ *clove crushed garlic*　　$\frac{1}{4}$ *tsp. salt*　　$\frac{1}{4}$ *tsp. freshly-ground pepper*
Good pinch of ground ginger　　1 *Tbs. finely chopped onion*
2 *Tbs. olive oil*　　4 *Tbs. lemon juice*

Mix together and leave to infuse for several hours or overnight. Strain before using.

Ask the butcher to bone the shoulder of lamb. Roll it up as tightly and neatly as possible with the skin side outside. Tie tightly with fine string at about $1\frac{1}{2}$ in. (4 cm.) intervals. Then take a long piece of string and tie the roll lengthwise, looping the string round each of the other ties in turn, on both sides. Put the meat on the spit making sure the weight is evenly distributed either side of the rod.

Roast at high heat until the meat is browned and then reduce the heat to finish cooking. Brush with the strained sauce at the beginning and several times during cooking.

It is advisable to make sure that boned meat is thoroughly cooked through to the middle to reduce the risk of infection which may be caused during the boning process. This is particularly important if the meat is being cooked to serve cold.

SPIT-ROASTED LOIN OF VEAL

Cooking Time 30–35 mins. per lb., stuffed weight.
Quantities Allow the equivalent of one good-sized chop per person.

> *Boned loin of veal*
> *Veal forcemeat (see below) or other stuffing*
> *Thinly sliced streaky bacon*

Spread the meat out flat, boned side uppermost. Spread with the stuffing and roll up tightly. Push several small skewers through to keep it in shape while you finish tying it. Wrap bacon rashers round to cover it completely, tying each rasher firmly with fine white string. Then tie a long piece of string lengthwise round the joint, looping it under each of the other ties. Remove the skewers. Put on the spit making sure the weight is evenly distributed.

Cook at high heat until the meat begins to brown and then more slowly to finish.

Alternative method
Instead of the stuffing use a mixture of chopped bacon and fresh chopped herbs. Omit the bacon wrapping but baste frequently with oil to keep the surface moist during cooking.

VEAL FORCEMEAT

Quantities for 4–6.

> 2 *oz. fresh breadcrumbs* (⅜ *c. or* 50 *g.*)
> 2 *oz. prepared suet* (50 *g.*)   *Pinch of grated nutmeg or mace*
> 1 *tsp. dried thyme or savory*   1 *egg, beaten*
> ½ *tsp. grated lemon rind*   1 *Tbs. chopped parsley*
> ½ *tsp. salt   Pinch of pepper   Milk to mix*

Mix all the ingredients together with milk, if necessary, to moisten and bind together.

15 Barbecues

Some authorities claim that the word barbecue comes from the Spanish 'barbacon' which was an iron grid placed over a fire to hold meat for drying and smoking, the name later coming to be used for an iron grid on which a whole animal was roasted.

Others say it comes from the French 'barbe à queue' meaning 'beard to tail' and signifies the dressing and roasting of a whole animal.

In the United States of America the name was adopted for an outdoor party at which a whole animal, such as an ox or pig, is roasted on a spit. This method of cooking for a lot of people outdoors is old and used in many countries of the world.

Now we have barbecue units, which are portable grills for outdoor cooking on patio or terrace, or ones suitable for packing in the car and taking for picnics or camping. Thus the word barbecue has come to mean almost any kind of outdoor cooking which entails grilling and, more recently, spit-roasting. Some of this barbecue apparatus is quite small with a simple gridiron for grills, others are large elaborate grills combined with mechanical spit-roasters and fittings for kebab skewers. Most of these units use charcoal for fuel, and the degree of heat is controlled by the size of the fire.

Many people build permanent barbecues in their gardens. These are usually of brick or stone with iron grids over the top of the fire to take meat or fish for grilling, a frying pan, or a boiling pot. Wood is the usual fuel.

SUITABLE FOODS FOR BARBECUE COOKING

Grills

Any of those on pages 133–42 can equally well be cooked on a barbecue grill. Large pieces of meat, and whole fish, can be placed across the iron bars above the fire, but for small pieces it is sometimes a help to use one of the old-fashioned wire hand-grills which were used in the days of domestic coal and wood ranges. These grip the food firmly and can be placed across the iron bars and turned over by means of the long handle.

Kebabs and Brochettes
Any of those on pages 67–79.

Some large portable barbecue units with a revolving spit have attachments for kebab skewers. If these are not available kebabs can be cooked by placing the skewers across the grid bars and turning them occasionally as they cook.

Spit-Roasting
For general directions see page 143.

Toasted Sandwiches
See pages 154–7.

For these you generally need a wire hand-grill as described under 'Grills', above, otherwise cook the sandwiches in a little fat in a frying pan.

Vegetables
For grilled vegetables, see pages 188–9.

They are usually more satisfactory if fastened on skewers as with kebabs, or cook them in a frying pan. Potatoes and other root vegetables can be wrapped in foil and cooked on the grill grid or, in the case of a wood fire, in the ashes; or boil them in a pan on the grid.

Some salads to serve with grills and spit roasts will be found on pages 183–7.

Sauces
For basting sauces see pages 167–8.
For sauces to serve with meat and fish, see pages 168–181.

Fruit
For Fruit Kebabs, see pages 89–90.

16 Grilled and Toasted Sandwiches and Snacks

These can be made on any kind of grill and are excellent for side table cooking. The ingredients can be prepared in advance and these delicious snacks made as required, and eaten really fresh which is the best way.

For those who don't like a lot of bread, open sandwiches are better than the ordinary toasted ones, see pages 154–7.

Almost any filling can be used, but the sandwich needs a topping suitable for grilling, for example, thin slices of cheese; grated cheese; thin rashers of bacon; chopped bacon; or sliced raw tomato. The topping shouldn't be too thick as its purpose is to protect the rest of the filling from burning, while at the same time allowing it to become hot.

Any bread can be used. Sometimes it is toasted first, on one side, while with other mixtures untoasted bread is used (see the recipes).

CHEESE, EGG AND BACON

Cooking Time 4–5 mins.   *Quantities* for 4.

2 eggs

Beat until light.

8 oz. grated cheese (250 g.)   *1 tsp. Worcester sauce*
1 tsp. paprika pepper   *½ tsp. dry mustard*

Add to the egg and mix well.

4 slices of bread toasted on one side

Spread the mixture on the untoasted side.

2–4 rashers diced bacon

Cover the tops with diced bacon and grill under a medium heat until the bacon is cooked and the cheese browned. Serve hot.

CHEESE AND SARDINE

Cooking Time 5–10 mins.　　*Quantities* for 4.

4 *oz. sardines* (125 *g.*)　　*Lemon juice*　　*Curry powder*

Mash the sardines, including the oil, and season to taste.

4 *slices bread*　　4 *slices cheese*

Toast the bread on one side. Spread the untoasted side with the sardine mixture and cover with the cheese. Grill slowly until the cheese is melted and brown.

Lettuce leaves　　*Sliced tomato or red pepper*

Use these to garnish the sandwiches and serve hot.

CHEESE, TOMATO AND BACON

Cooking Time 10–15 mins.　　*Quantities* for 4.

4 *slices toasted bread*　　4 *slices mature cheese*
2 *tomatoes*　　4 *small rashers bacon*

Flavouring: Curry powder; made mustard; anchovy essence; Marmite; Worcester sauce; paprika pepper.

Put a slice of cheese on each piece of toast. Sprinkle or spread the cheese with the chosen flavouring. Cover with slices of tomato and then with the bacon diced or cut in strips. Grill slowly until the bacon is cooked.

CRAB

Cooking Time about 5 mins.　　*Quantities* for 4.

4 *slices of bread toasted on one side*
4 *oz. cooked crab meat* (125 *g.*)
Mayonnaise or salad dressing to moisten

Mix the crab meat and mayonnaise or dressing and spread it on the untoasted side of the bread.

4 *thin slices cheese*

Put on top of the crab and grill slowly until the cheese is melted.

EGG AND HADDOCK

Cooking Time about 10 mins.　　*Quantities* for 4.

4 *eggs*　　2 *Tbs. milk*　　8 *oz. cooked flaked haddock* (250 *g.*)
1 *Tbs. lemon juice*　　*Pepper*　　*Chopped parsley*

Beat the eggs to mix and add the other ingredients.

½ oz. butter or margarine (1 Tbs.)

Melt in a small pan and scramble the egg mixture. This stage can be done in advance and the mixture refrigerated until required.

4 slices bread   4 thin slices cheese

Toast the bread on one side and spread the other side with the filling. Cover with the cheese. Grill slowly until the cheese has melted and begun to brown.

HERRING ROE

Quantities for 4 large sandwiches.

8 oz. canned soft herring roes (250 g.)
2 oz. softened butter or margarine (50 g.)
2 tsp. French mustard
1 Tbs. Worcester sauce   Pepper
Lemon juice

Drain the roes and empty them into a basin. Mash to a smooth paste with the other ingredients, seasoning to taste with pepper and lemon juice.

4 large slices bread
1 can plain flat anchovy fillets (2 oz. or 56 g.)

Toast the bread on both sides. Rinse and drain the anchovies. Spread the mixture on the toast and put 3 anchovy fillets on top of each. Grill until the mixture begins to brown and is well heated. Serve hot.

WELSH RAREBIT (GRILLED)

Cooking Time 5–10 mins.   *Quantities* for 4.

4 oz. strong Cheddar or Cheshire cheese (125 g.)
½ Tbs. cornflour   ½ tsp. made mustard   Salt and pepper
2½ Tbs. milk, or use ale, or half sherry and half milk.

Grate the cheese and mix it with the other ingredients. This may be done in advance and the mixture stored in a covered dish in the refrigerator.

4 slices of bread   Butter for spreading (optional)

Toast the bread on both sides. Spread with butter if liked but this is not really necessary. Spread with the cheese mixture and grill under a moderate heat until the cheese is melted and brown on top. Serve at once.

ANCHOVY RAREBIT

Instead of all milk use 2 Tbs. milk and ½ Tbs. anchovy essence.

or

Put some rinsed anchovy fillets on top and return to the grill to warm them.

SARDINE RAREBIT

Put a couple of sardines on each portion and return to the grill to make them hot.

WALNUT RAREBIT

Add 2 oz. finely-chopped walnuts (50 g.) to the Welsh Rarebit mixture.

YORKSHIRE RAREBIT

Put a thin slice of ham on the toast before spreading on the Welsh Rarebit mixture. Grill slowly until brown.

BLUE CHEESE RAREBIT

Quantities for 2–4.

> *4 oz. grated or mashed blue-vein cheese (125 g.)*
> *A few grains of cayenne pepper*
> *3 Tbs. mayonnaise*
> *2 oz. soft butter or margarine (50 g.)*
> *1 oz. chopped walnuts (25 g.)*

Mix all together thoroughly and leave in a cold place to become firm before using.

> *2–4 slices toast*

Spread the cheese mixture on the toast and grill until the top is brown. Serve hot.

TOASTED SANDWICHES

The best equipment for making these is a horizontal toaster or grill.

Toasted sandwiches make excellent quick snack meals, especially if served with a salad to follow or with fresh fruit. Most of the ingredients can be prepared in advance and the family can toast their own sandwiches freshly as required.

154

Ordinary machine-sliced white bread is usually the most satisfactory, fairly thinly sliced, though this is a matter of taste. It can be fresh or stale but not dry.

The chosen filling is put between unbuttered slices and it is the outsides which are buttered. For this you can brush on melted butter or margarine or give a very thin spreading of softened butter or one of the very soft margarines. The covering should be thin but even, otherwise results will be disappointing. Crusts can be removed or not according to taste.

The easiest way of assembling one of these sandwiches is to put one slice of bread, buttered side down on the grill rack, add the filling and then the top slice of buttered bread. This avoids handling the greasy surfaces. Toast fairly slowly so that the bread browns evenly and the filling heats through. Turn with tongs or a fish slice.

Below I have given some of the fillings I particularly like but any others are suitable provided there is plenty of filling and it is not too dry.

If you prefer less bread with sandwiches, open grilled sandwiches are the alternative. For these, see page 151.

CHEESE

One of the very best and one of the easiest to prepare. For each sandwich have a thick slice of strong cheese, spread it with mustard and toast slowly so that the cheese begins to melt by the time the bread is browned.

CHEESE AND CHUTNEY

Spread the slice of strong cheese with sweet chutney.

CHEESE AND ANCHOVY

For 2 large sandwiches melt 2 oz. (50 g.) of butter or margarine and mix in 2 tsp. of anchovy essence. Use this to brush the bread with. For the filling use a thick slice of well-flavoured cheese.

Alternative

Spread the cheese with anchovy essence or anchovy paste and brush or spread the bread with butter or margarine in the usual way.

CHEESE AND ONION

For 2 large sandwiches grate 4 oz. cheese (125 g.) and mix with grated raw onion to taste and enough boiling water to make a spreadable paste.

Alternative
In the electric blender put the cheese, cut up, 1 slice of onion and about 4 Tbs. boiling water. Blend smooth.

LOBSTER OR CRAB

Allow about 1–2 oz. (25–50 g.) lobster or crab meat, fresh or canned (dressed crab will do). Mix this with mayonnaise or salad dressing to moisten well.

MEAT

Allow 1–2 oz. cooked or canned meat per large sandwich (25–50 g.). Use minced meat or poultry and moisten it with plenty of chutney or bottled sauce.

CHEESE SPREAD

This is to make and store in the refrigerator for later use.

Quantities for 2–4 sandwiches.

> *4 oz. strong cheese, grated (125 g.)*
> *1 oz. soft butter or margarine (25 g.)*
> *Pinch of paprika pepper*
> *2 Tbs. sherry*

Mix all together and use for toasted sandwiches or use in place of a Welsh Rarebit. Toast bread one side, spread with the mixture and then grill to brown it.

FISH AND CHEESE

Cooking Time about 5 mins.   *Quantities* for 4.

> *4–6 oz. cooked or canned fish (125–175 g.)*
> *Bottled sauce, mayonnaise or sour cream*

Remove any skin and hard bones from the fish, flake or mash it and add enough sauce to bind the flakes together but not make it wet.

> *4 slices strong cheese   French mustard*
> *8 slices bread   Soft margarine or butter*

Make the sandwiches with a layer of fish, then cheese, and spread the cheese with mustard. Spread the outsides of the sandwich with a thin covering of margarine or butter. Toast slowly so that the cheese has time to begin to melt and the outsides become brown. Serve hot.

SARDINE AND CHEESE

Quantities for 4–6 sandwiches.

> 3–4 *oz. can sardines* (125 g.)

Mash the sardines with the oil in the can.

> 4 *oz. melted butter or margarine* (125 g.)
> 1 *slice of onion, chopped finely*   2 *Tbs. lemon juice*
> 2 *oz. grated cheese* (50 g.) $\frac{1}{4}$ *tsp. paprika pepper*
> *Salt and pepper*

Mix all together thoroughly and leave to become cold. Spread between thin slices of bread.

> *Soft margarine*

Spread the outsides of the sandwiches with a very thin layer of margarine and toast slowly until golden brown and heated through.

SARDINE AND OLIVE

Quantities for 4–6 sandwiches.

> 3–4 *oz. can sardines in oil* (125 g.)   4 *stuffed olives*

Mash the sardines with the oil. Chop the olives finely.

> 3 *Tbs. mayonnaise*   1 *Tbs. lemon juice*
> *Pinch of garlic salt*   *Pinch of pepper*
> 2 *oz. melted butter or margarine* (50 g.)

Mix all together and leave to become cold before using. Spread between slices of unbuttered bread.

> *Soft margarine*

Spread the outsides of the sandwiches with a very thin layer of margarine and toast slowly until golden brown on the outside and heated through.

SMOKED COD'S ROE

Quantities for 6–8 large sandwiches.

> 8 *oz. smoked cod's roe* (250 g.)

Remove any skin from the outside and mash the roe thoroughly. If it is at all lumpy, rub it through a sieve.

2 *Tbs. lemon juice*
Pinch *of cayenne pepper*

½ *tsp. dry mustard*
About ¼ *pt. olive oil* (½ *c. or* 150 *ml.*)

Add to the roe and beat thoroughly using enough oil to make it a soft spread. Sandwich unbuttered slices of bread with the filling.

Soft margarine

Spread the outsides of the sandwiches with a very thin layer of margarine. Toast slowly until golden brown on both sides.

GRIDDLE SANDWICHES

For the electric frypan.

Use fairly thinly sliced white bread, machine-sliced for preference. The filling can be just a thick slice of cheese spread with mustard, or any of the fillings on pages 155–7.

Put the filling in the unbuttered bread. Brush one of the outsides with melted butter or margarine.

Heat the frypan to about 340° (170°C) and put in the sandwiches, buttered side down. Brush the top sides with more melted butter or margarine. Cook for 4–5 mins. or until the sandwiches are brown underneath, turn (using tongs or a fish slice), and brown the other side.

CROQUE MONSIEUR

Griddle sandwiches for the frypan.

Cooking Time 10–15 mins.   *Quantities* for 4.

> 8 *thin slices white bread*
> 4 *slices Emmental cheese a little smaller than the bread*
> 4 *slices cooked ham the same size as the cheese*
> *Softened butter or margarine*

Spread one side of four pieces of bread very thinly with butter or margarine and put them butter side down in the frypan. Put on the cheese and then the ham. Butter the remaining pieces of bread and put on top of the ham, buttered side up.

Turn the control to about 340° (170°C) and cook until brown underneath, turn (using tongs or a fish slice), and brown the other side. By this time the cheese should just be beginning to melt. Serve hot.

158

These are all snacks which can be cooked on the side table on a hot-plate or burner and some in the electric frypan. You also need a portable toaster, or grill for the toast.

ANCHOVY TOASTS

Suitable for hot snacks at a buffet, for a savoury at the end of a meal, or for a snack meal followed by cheese and salad.

Cooking Time a few mins.   *Quantities* for 4.

4 slices bread   *Butter*

Toast the bread on both sides and spread with butter.

1–2 Tbs. finely chopped onion   *2 Tbs. chopped parsley*

Sprinkle this on the toast.

1 small can of anchovy fillets (2 oz. or 56 g.)
Lemon juice   *Cayenne pepper or paprika pepper*

Rinse the anchovy fillets to remove some of the salt. Drain and put several on each piece of toast. Sprinkle with lemon juice and pepper and put back under the grill to heat the anchovies.

Either serve whole, or trim off the crusts and cut the toast in fingers each with a piece of anchovy on it.

BAKED BEANS AND CHEESE

Suitable for hotplate or frypan.

Cooking Time a few mins.   *Quantities* for 4.

1 lb. can baked beans in tomato sauce (454 g.)
4 oz. grated cheese (125 g.)
2 canned pimientos, drained and chopped
1 tsp. Worcester sauce

Put all in a saucepan or in the frypan and cook over a gentle heat until the cheese is melted and the whole mixture hot. Electric frypan 300° (150°C).

4 slices toast or 4 fresh rolls

Either pour the mixture over the toast or serve it in small hot dishes with the rolls handed separately.

Alternative
Serve without any bread but with a tossed green salad.

BEANS AND MUSHROOMS

Suitable for a hotplate or electric frypan.

Cooking Time 10 mins.   *Quantities* for 3.

> *2 Tbs. finely-chopped onion*
> *1½ oz. butter or margarine (45 g.)*
> *8 oz. sliced mushrooms (250 g.)*

Heat the butter or margarine in a large frying pan or heat the electric frypan at about 360° (180°C) and then add the fat. Fry the onion and mushrooms until the onion begins to brown.

> *16 oz. can baked beans in tomato sauce (½ kg.)*
> *1 Tbs. Worcester sauce   1 tsp. soy sauce*
> *Salt to taste   Dried marjoram to taste*

Add to the pan and simmer until well heated. Taste for seasoning.

> *Chopped parsley   Toast or brown bread*

Serve sprinkled with plenty of chopped parsley and hand the toast or bread separately.

CRAB SCALLOPS

For the grill.

Cooking Time 5 mins.   *Quantities* for 4.

> *8 oz. crab meat (250 g.), fresh, canned or frozen*
> *4 Tbs. mayonnaise   1 Tbs. Worcester sauce*
> *½ tsp. made mustard*

Thaw frozen crab meat. Mix all ingredients together and put it into buttered scallop shells or small flat fireproof dishes. It is better in individual portions but can be made in one flat dish provided it is a suitable size for putting under the grill.

> *Buttered crumbs   Grated cheese*

Melt a little butter and mix fresh breadcrumbs into it to coat them. Use these, mixed with cheese, to sprinkle over the top of the crab. Heat under a moderate grill to warm through and brown the top. Serve hot.

160

Accompaniments
Fingers of toast or French bread and butter. Lemon wedges.

CREAM CHEESE AND WALNUT TOASTS

This is improved if the filling is made in advance and stored in the refrigerator to become firm.

Quantities for 3.

> 4 *small Gervais Petit Swiss cream cheeses*
> 2 *Tbs. double cream*

Mash the cheese and mix in the cream.

> 2 *Tbs. honey*

Add and mix in well.

> 2 *oz. walnuts* (50 *g.*), *finely chopped*

Add and mix in.

> 3 *slices toast*   *Butter*

Butter the toast lightly and spread the mixture on top. Garnish with walnut halves.

CREAMED MUSHROOMS

For hotplate or frypan.

Cooking Time a few mins.   *Quantities* for 4.

> 1 *oz. butter* (25 *g.*)   8 *oz. mushrooms* (250 *g.*)

Wash the mushrooms and slice them, not too finely. Heat the frypan at 360° (180°C) and when it is up to temperature, add the butter. When it melts fry the mushrooms, stirring with a wooden spoon for one minute. Turn the heat down a little.

> $\frac{1}{2}$ *tsp. salt*   *Pinch of freshly-ground pepper*
> 2 *Tbs. flour*

Sprinkle these over the mushrooms and mix quickly.

> $\frac{1}{4}$ *pt. milk* ($\frac{1}{2}$ *c. or* 150 *ml.*) $\frac{1}{4}$ *pt. double cream* ($\frac{1}{2}$ *c. or* 150 *ml.*)
> 1 *Tbs. lemon juice or sherry*

Add to the mushrooms, stir until boiling, and serve in small hot dishes.

Accompaniments
Fingers of hot buttered toast or brown bread and butter.

EGGS WITH CHEESE AND PARSLEY

Suitable for hotplate or frypan.

Quantities for 4–6.

2 *oz. butter* (50 *g.*)   2 *Tbs. chopped parsley*

Melt the butter and fry the parsley in it for a few seconds.

4 *oz. strong grated cheese* (125 *g.*)
½ *pt. dry white wine or cider* (1 *c. or* 250 *ml.*)

Remove the pan from the heat or turn down the heat. Add cheese and wine or cider and stir until the cheese is melted.

8 *eggs*

Break the eggs into the cheese mixture one at a time, mixing each in with the stirrer or a small whisk. Combine each with the mixture before adding the next. Heat and stir all the time until it thickens.

Fingers of toast or fried bread

Serve the egg mixture on hot plates and hand the toast or bread separately. If fried bread is used it can be cooked first and kept hot while the eggs are cooked.

FRENCH FINGERS

For serving with salads, soups or any savoury dishes, or by themselves for a cocktail savoury.

Cooking Time about 5 mins.

Slices of thin bread and butter   Finely-grated strong cheese

Sprinkle the bread and butter generously and evenly with the cheese. Press with a palette knife to make it stick. Cut the bread in fingers and grill fairly slowly until brown and crisp. Serve warm or hot.

HAM RAREBIT

Suitable for a hotplate.

Cooking Time a few mins.   *Quantities* for 4–6.

2 *oz. butter or margarine* (50 *g.*)   2 *Tbs. flour*
1 *tsp. dry mustard*

Melt the fat in a saucepan and add the dry ingredients, mix until smooth.

½ pt. single cream (1 c. or 250 ml.)   2 tsp. Worcester sauce
2 oz. grated Cheddar cheese (50 g.)   2 Tbs. sherry

Add the cream gradually and then the other ingredients. Stir and cook gently until the cheese is melted.

6 oz. diced cooked ham (175 g.)

Add and heat for a few minutes.

4–6 slices toast, buttered and sprinkled with paprika pepper

Pour the rarebit on the toast and serve.

HONEY DATE AND WALNUT TOAST

Quantities for 4.

2 oz. dates (50 g.)   2 oz. walnuts (50 g.)

Chop the dates small and mince the walnuts finely or pulverise them in the electric blender.

2 oz. softened butter (50 g.)   4 Tbs. honey

Mix together and then add the dates and honey.

4 slices toast   Butter

Make the toast and butter it lightly. Spread with the honey mixture and garnish with a piece of date or walnut. Serve hot.

LEMON BUTTER TOAST

Quantities for 3–4 slices of a large loaf.

1 tsp. lemon juice   1 tsp. grated lemon rind
1 oz. butter or margarine (25 g.)

Soften the butter by warming it, or use soft margarine. Combine with the juice and rind.

3–4 slices of bread

Toast one side of the bread. Spread the untoasted side with the butter mixture, not quite to the edges. Toast slowly until golden brown. Trim off the crusts. Cut in fingers and serve.

RAREBIT WITH GHERKINS

Suitable for a hotplate.

Quantities for 4–6.

6 Tbs. milk   2 oz. butter or margarine (50 g.)
8 oz. grated Cheshire or Cheddar cheese (250 g.)

Put these in a small pan and stir over a moderate heat until the cheese melts.

2 *tsp. vinegar* 2 *tsp. made mustard*
Salt and pepper 4 *Tbs. chopped gherkins*

Add to the cheese mixture.

2 *tsp. potato flour or cornflour blended with a little cold water*

Mix into the cheese and stir until it thickens.

4–6 *slices toast, spread with butter or margarine*

Pour the mixture on the toast and serve at once.

SCRAMBLED EGGS WITH VEGETABLES AND CHEESE

Suitable for a hotplate.

Cooking Time about 5 mins. *Quantities* for 4.

6 *eggs* 2 *Tbs. cream*

Whisk together thoroughly.

1 *oz. butter* (25 *g.*)

Heat in a small pan and add the eggs. Turn down the heat and cook gently.

4 *oz. cooked diced vegetables* (125 *g.*)

When the egg begins to set, add the vegetables and stir in gently to mix well.

1 *oz. butter* (25 *g.*) 1 *tsp. French mustard*
2 *oz. grated cheese* (50 *g.*) *Salt and pepper to taste*

Add and mix in, heating until the butter melts but avoid over-cooking.

Bread and butter or toast

Serve the egg on a small hot plate and serve the bread or toast separately.

WELSH RAREBIT (FONDUE)

This is the kind to cook in a fondue pot or in a small pan on a hotplate. For the other kind of Welsh Rarebit, see page 153.

Cooking Time a few mins. *Quantities* for 2–3.

4 *oz. strong Cheddar cheese* (125 *g.*)
1 *oz. butter* (25 *g.*)
1 *tsp. made mustard or Worcester sauce* (*or both*)
1 *tsp. potato flour* 5 *Tbs. brown ale or stout*

Grate the cheese coarsely. Blend the potato flour with the ale or stout and put all the ingredients in the fondue pot or small pan. Cook gently, stirring all the time, until the cheese has melted and the mixture is smooth and bubbling.

2–3 slices freshly-made toast

Pour the mixture over the toast and serve.

17 Sauces

These are recipes for sauces mentioned throughout the book as suitable accompaniments for fondues, grills and other dishes.

BARBECUE BASTING SAUCES

Use these for keeping the surface of grilled foods moist and for adding flavour. They should be brushed over the food, or spooned over it. They can also be used as a marinade to give extra flavour to meat or fish.

BASIC BARBECUE SAUCE

Quantities for 4.

1 *tsp. dry mustard*	2 *Tbs. vinegar*
2 *tsp. Worcester sauce*	3 *Tbs. oil or melted butter*

Garlic Basting Sauce
Crush a clove of garlic and infuse it in the Basic Barbecue sauce for several hours. Strain before use.

Herb Basting Sauce
Add crushed dried herbs to the Basic Barbecue sauce. Use just one kind or a mixture. Best are thyme, marjoram, bay leaf or rosemary.

ANCHOVY BASTING SAUCE

Quantities for 4.

2 *Tbs. Worcester sauce*	2 *Tbs. tomato ketchup*
1 *tsp. anchovy essence*	1 *Tbs. made mustard*
½ *clove finely-chopped garlic*	

Mix together and use, or, if preferred, infuse for several hours and then strain out the garlic.

GINGER AND LEMON BASTING SAUCE

Quantities for 4.

½ *clove crushed garlic*	¼ *tsp. salt*
¼ *tsp. freshly-ground pepper*	¼ *tsp. ground ginger*
1 *Tbs. finely-chopped onion*	2 *Tbs. olive oil*
4 *Tbs. lemon juice*	

Mix together and leave to infuse for several hours or overnight. Strain before using.

WINE BASTING SAUCE

For the wine use red or white wine, sherry or vermouth. Mix it with an equal quantity of oil and infuse fresh herbs in it for several hours before using. Use chopped marjoram, thyme or rosemary, crushed garlic and a bay leaf. Strain before using.

MAYONNAISE

This is very easy to make provided you remember to have both the oil and the egg at room temperature. If either is too cold, the mixture will tend to separate. Use a small basin for mixing and either a little wooden spoon or a small egg beater. If it is winter-time make sure the bowl is not freezing cold.

2 *egg yolks*	½ *tsp. salt*
Pinch of cayenne pepper	1 *Tbs. vinegar*
½ *tsp. dry mustard*	

Mix these smooth.

½ *pt. salad oil or olive oil* (1 *c.* or 250 *ml.*)

Stir the egg mixture vigorously, or whisk, while adding the oil drop by drop from a tablespoon held in the other hand. Let the drops fall in fairly continuously, but make sure it mixes in as soon as added, otherwise go more slowly with adding the oil. When about half has been mixed in, add the rest a tablespoon at a time making sure each spoonful is mixed in before adding the next. Add

1 *Tbs. vinegar or lemon juice to taste*

Store in a cool place. For a meat fondue it may be flavoured in any of the ways given below.

MAYONNAISE AURORE

Quantities for 4 or more.

> ¼ *pt. mayonnaise* (½ *c. or 150 ml.*)
> 1 *Tbs. double cream*
> ½–1 *Tbs. concentrated tomato purée*
> *A dash of Worcester sauce*

Combine ingredients using enough tomato to give a pink sauce.

CURRY MAYONNAISE

Quantities for 4 or more.

> ¼ *pt. mayonnaise* (½ *c. or 150 ml.*)   1 *Tbs. curry powder*

Whisk the curry into the mayonnaise, adding more if a hotter sauce
is preferred.

FENNEL MAYONNAISE

(for fish fondue and grilled fish)

Quantities for 4 or more.

> ¼ *pt. mayonnaise* (½ *c. or 150 ml.*)
> 1–2 *Tbs. chopped fresh fennel leaves*

Chop the fennel just before serving the sauce and combine well with
the mayonnaise.

GARLIC MAYONNAISE

Quantities for 4.

> 2 *cloves garlic*   4 *Tbs. mayonnaise*

Pound the garlic using the flat side of a knife and mix with the
mayonnaise.

PAPRIKA MAYONNAISE

Quantities for 4 or more.

> ¼ *pt. mayonnaise* (½ *c. or 150 ml.*)   1 *tsp. paprika pepper*

Whisk the pepper into the mayonnaise until there is a good flavour
of paprika and a good pink colour.

RÉMOULADE SAUCE

Quantities for 4 or more.

> $\frac{1}{4}$ *pt. mayonnaise* ($\frac{1}{2}$ *c. or 150 ml.*)
> 1–2 *tsp. made mustard*
> 1 *tsp. chopped gherkins*   1 *tsp. chopped capers*
> 1 *tsp. chopped fines herbes* (*parsley, tarragon, chervil*)
> $\frac{1}{2}$ *tsp. anchovy essence*

Mix all together making sure there is plenty of mustard flavour.

TARTARE SAUCE

Quantities for 4 or more.

> $\frac{1}{2}$ *tsp. finely-chopped onion*
> 1 *Tbs. finely-chopped gherkins or capers*
> $\frac{1}{4}$ *pt. mayonnaise* ($\frac{1}{2}$ *c. or 150 ml.*)
> *A little wine or wine vinegar*

Mix the ingredients together adding the wine or vinegar only if the mixture needs thinning.

SAVOURY BUTTERS

These are very useful sauces for meat fondues and for grills. They can be made in advance and stored in the refrigerator or in the freezer.

Allow $\frac{1}{2}$–1 oz. butter (1–2 Tbs.) per portion depending on how it is to be used. For a meat fondue have the butter softish, at room temperature, but for grills it can be in firm pats.

ANCHOVY BUTTER

> 4 *oz. softened butter* (125 *g.*)   2 *tsp. anchovy essence*

Combine thoroughly.

CURRY BUTTER

> 4 *oz. softened butter* (125 *g.*)   1 *tsp. curry powder*
> $\frac{1}{2}$ *tsp. salt*   *Few drops of onion juice*

Combine thoroughly. To make onion juice, grate a cut onion finely.

GARLIC BUTTER

4 oz. softened butter (125 g.)
1 small clove of garlic, minced

Cream the butter until light, add the garlic and leave to stand for an hour or more before using.

Alternative Method
Pound the butter and garlic together in a mortar.

MAÎTRE D'HÔTEL OR PARSLEY BUTTER

4 oz. softened butter (125 g.)   *2 Tbs. chopped parsley*
Lemon juice to taste

Beat together to a smooth cream. Form into pats and refrigerate until required. Put the firm pats on grilled fish or meat, to melt and make a sauce.

MINT BUTTER

4 oz. softened butter (125 g.)   ½ *pt. mint leaves* (1 *c. or* 250 *ml.*)
½ *pt. parsley sprigs* (1 *c. or* 250 *ml.*)

Wash the mint and parsley leaves and boil them in the smallest possible amount of water until they are pulpy. Rub through a sieve. Work into the butter until smooth.

MUSTARD BUTTER

4 oz. softened butter (125 g.)   *2 Tbs. French mustard*

Combine thoroughly.

PAPRIKA BUTTER

1 Tbs. chopped onion
½ *oz. butter for frying* (1 *Tbs.*)
4 oz. softened butter (125 g.)
Good pinch of paprika pepper

Fry the chopped onion in the ½ oz. of butter, adding the paprika during frying. Cool. Work into the butter and then rub through a sieve. Add more paprika if liked.

TARRAGON BUTTER

4 *oz. softened butter* (125 *g.*)
$\frac{1}{4}$ *pt. tarragon leaves* ($\frac{1}{2}$ *c. or* 150 *ml.*)

Blanch the tarragon leaves by pouring boiling water over them. Then plunge them in cold water, drain, and dry by pressing between paper towels. Chop the leaves, work them into the butter and finally rub through a sieve to make the mixture smooth. This makes a well-flavoured green butter.

APPLE SAUCE

Cooking Time $\frac{1}{2}$ hr.   *Quantities* for 4.

1 *lb. cooking apples* ($\frac{1}{2}$ *kg.*)   2 *oz. sugar* (4 *Tbs. or* 50 *g.*)

Peel, core and slice the apples and cook them in a saucepan with just enough water to prevent burning. Cook to a pulp. If a smooth sauce is wanted, rub the pulp through a nylon sieve or put in the electric blender. Add the sugar and re-heat. Serve hot.

BÉARNAISE SAUCE

Cooking Time a few mins.   *Quantities* for 4–6.

1 *tsp. finely-chopped shallot or onion*
A sprig each of tarragon and chervil
Pinch of salt   5 *Tbs. white wine vinegar*

Cut the tarragon and chervil up roughly, put all the ingredients in the top of a double boiler and boil over direct heat until the liquid is reduced to about a dessertspoonful. Remove from the heat and cool a little.

2 *egg yolks*   3 *oz. melted butter* (75 *g.*)

Add egg yolks to the vinegar and herbs and put the pan over boiling water. Whisk to mix the egg yolks and then add the butter and continue whisking until the sauce thickens. Rub it through a small nylon sieve and don't heat any more or it will separate. But don't despair if this does happen. Cool the sauce by standing the pan in cold water and whisking hard to make it smooth again.

1 *tsp. each of chopped chervil and tarragon*
Cayenne pepper

Add to the strained sauce and serve just warm, or cold.

BÉCHAMEL SAUCE

Cooking Time 15–20 mins.   *Quantities* for 4–8 depending on how it is used.

1 *pt. milk* (2 *c.* or ½ *l.*)   *Piece of celery*
1 *shallot or small onion*   1 *bay leaf*
Piece of carrot   10 *peppercorns*

Peel the onion or shallot and clean the other vegetables. Put all ingredients in a pan and bring to the boil. Remove from the heat and leave to infuse for 5 mins. Strain.

1½ *oz. butter or margarine* (45 *g.*)
1½ *oz. flour* (4½ *Tbs. or* 45 *g.*)

Melt the butter or margarine in a saucepan and stir in the flour. Cook gently until it looks crumbly. Remove from the heat and gradually whisk in the strained milk, whisking until smooth. Return to the heat and stir until it boils. Boil gently for 5 mins.

Salt   4 *Tbs. single cream*

Season to taste and add the cream just before serving.

BRETON SAUCE

Quantities for 4.

1 *Tbs. French mustard*   2 *egg yolks*   1 *Tbs. wine vinegar*
¼ *tsp. salt*   *Pinch of pepper*

Mix together until well blended.

2 *oz. butter* (50 *g.*)

Soften until almost melted and then whisk into the egg mixture until the sauce is the consistency of mayonnaise.

2 *Tbs. chopped fresh herbs or to taste*

Mix into the sauce and serve.

CHIVES SAUCE

Make Breton Sauce, above, and for the herbs use finely-chopped chives to taste.

CHUTNEY SAUCE, SWEET

Quantities. For a fondue sauce, allow 1–2 Tbs. per person.

To make a smooth sauce either rub the chutney through a nylon sieve or put it in the blender and mix smooth. If necessary thin down to a suitable consistency with lemon juice or vinegar.

CRANBERRY SAUCE

Cooking Time 10 mins.   *Quantities* for 4.

8 *oz. cranberries (2½ c. or 250 g.)*
¼ *pt. water (½ c. or 150 ml.)*

Boil the cranberries in the water, crushing them with a spoon as they begin to soften. When they are quite soft rub them through a nylon sieve or cool a little and mix smooth in the electric blender. Strain after blending to make sure it is quite smooth.

4 *oz. sugar (½ c. or 125 g.)*

Add the sugar, re-heat, and stir until the sugar dissolves. Serve hot or cold, thinning as necessary with water.

CUMBERLAND SAUCE

Quantities for 8 or more.

4 *Tbs. red currant jelly*
8 *Tbs. port wine or red wine (4 fl. oz. or 120 ml.)*

Put in a small pan and heat gently, stirring to dissolve the jelly.

1 *tsp. grated orange rind*   1 *tsp. grated lemon rind*
2 *Tbs. orange juice*   1 *Tbs. lemon juice*
1 *tsp. dry mustard*   *Pinch of ground ginger*
Cayenne pepper

Mix together and add to the melted jelly. Allow to become cold before using.

This sauce keeps very well, especially in a covered jar in the refrigerator.

CURRY SAUCE, COLD

Quantities for 4–6.

4 *Tbs. peeled and finely-grated apple*   4 *Tbs. double cream*
Curry powder to taste   *Salt to taste*

Mix all together thoroughly by hand or in an electric blender, in which case there is no need to grate the apple first, just blend long enough to break it up finely. Use plenty of curry powder. The combination of curry and raw apple gives a pleasant, nutty taste to the sauce, particularly good with a beef fondue.

CURRY SAUCE, HOT

Cooking Time 15–20 mins.　　*Quantities* for 4.

1 *small onion*　　½ *oz. butter* (15 g.)

Skin and slice the onion finely. Heat the butter and fry the onion slowly, with the lid on the pan, until it is tender but not brown.

1 *Tbs. curry powder*

Add and cook for a minute longer.

¼ *pt. stock* (½ *c. or* 150 *ml.*)
¼ *pt. double cream* (½ *c. or* 150 *ml.*)

Add stock and boil for a few minutes. Just before serving add the cream and boil until it thickens a little. Taste, and add salt if necessary.

This is not meant to be a thick sauce.

EGG SAUCE (for grilled fish)

Quantities for 4.

2 *eggs*

Hard-boil, shell and mash, or chop.

4 *oz. butter* (125 g.)　　½–1 *tsp. curry powder*
¼–½ *tsp. paprika pepper*

Melt the butter and add the egg and flavourings. Mix well and make sure that it is hot before serving.

ESPAGNOLE OR MADEIRA SAUCE

This may be made in advance and stored in the refrigerator or the freezer.

Cooking Time 1¼ hrs.　　*Quantities* for 6 or more.

2 *oz. butter* (50 g.)　　2 *oz. chopped ham or bacon* (50 g.)

Heat the butter and fry the ham or bacon in it for a few minutes.

1 *medium-sized onion*　　1 *small carrot*
6 *mushrooms or an equivalent amount of stalks*

Peel the onion and scrape the carrot, chop them. Wash and chop the mushrooms. Add to the pan and continue frying until the vegetables begin to brown.

175

1 *oz. flour* (3 *Tbs. or* 25 *g.*)

Sprinkle into the pan and stir and cook until it begins to brown.

1 *pt. brown stock* (2 *c. or* ½ *l.*) *or use meat cubes*
2 *Tbs. concentrated tomato purée*

Add to the pan and stir until it boils. Boil gently for an hour, adding more stock if it seems to need it. Strain the sauce through a fine sieve.

4 *Tbs. sherry or madeira*   *Salt and pepper*

Add the wine, season to taste and re-heat.

FRENCH DRESSING

Quantities for 4.

1½ *Tbs. olive oil*   *Pinch of dry mustard*
Pinch of sugar   *Pinch of pepper*   ¼ *tsp. salt*
½ *Tbs. vinegar* (*wine, cider, tarragon or other flavour*)

Mix the oil and seasonings and add the vinegar. Stir before using.

HERB SAUCE

Quantities for 6 or more.

½ *small onion*   *A good sprig of parsley*
A few tarragon leaves   *A sprig of thyme*
A few marjoram leaves

Skin the onion and chop very finely. Wash, dry and chop the herbs.

6 *Tbs. olive oil*   2 *Tbs. wine vinegar*
3 *Tbs. lemon juice*   1 *tsp. sugar*
½ *tsp. salt*   *Pinch of pepper*

Mix all together, and add the onion and herbs. Leave to stand a while before serving. Stir before using.

Alternative Method
Put all ingredients, whole onion and uncut herbs in the electric blender and mix until the herbs and onion are finely chopped.

HOLLANDAISE SAUCE

Quantities for 4 or more, depending on how used.

4 *oz. butter* (125 *g.*)   2 *egg yolks*   1 *Tbs. lemon juice*

Divide the butter into 3 portions and put one in a pan with the egg yolks and the lemon juice. Cook over hot water, stirring with a wire whisk until the butter is melted. Add the second piece of butter and whisk and heat until the sauce begins to thicken slightly. Add the third piece of butter.

2–3 Tbs. boiling water   ¼ tsp. salt   Few grains cayenne pepper

Add the boiling water to give the desired consistency (it is meant to be thin), and beat for 1 min. more. Add the seasonings and remove from the heat at once.

Should the mixture curdle add 2 Tbs. double cream or 2 Tbs. boiling water drop by drop, beating hard all the time.

If the sauce is not to be served at once keep it warm, not hot, or it will separate.

HORSERADISH SAUCE

Quantities for 4 or more.

4 Tbs. grated fresh horseradish   2 tsp. dry mustard
1 tsp. wine vinegar   ½ tsp. salt   Pinch of paprika pepper
¼ pt. sour or cultured cream or yogurt (½ c. or 150 ml.)

Mix all together, cover and store in the refrigerator until required.

HORSERADISH SAUCE (Quick)

Use bottled horseradish sauce diluted to a suitable consistency with fresh cream, cultured cream or yogurt.

KETCHUP AND CREAM SAUCE

Quantities for 4.

¼ pt. tomato ketchup (½ c. or 150 ml.)   1 tsp. Worcester sauce   1 Tbs. horseradish sauce   ½ Tbs. lemon juice
½ tsp. dry mustard   ¼ pt. double cream (½ c. or 150 ml.)

Mix all together until well blended. Serve cold.

LEMON SAUCE

Cooking Time 10–15 mins.   *Quantities* for 4 or more if used for a fondue.

2 egg yolks   2 Tbs. lemon juice

Beat together until thick.

½ *pt. warm stock* (1 *c. or* 250 *ml.*)
1 *tsp. potato flour blended with a little cold water*

Add to the eggs, put over boiling water and cook until the mixture thickens a little. It is meant to be a fairly thin sauce.

Salt and pepper

Season to taste and use hot or cold.

MINT SAUCE

Quantities for 4 or more.

¼ *c. of chopped fresh mint* (150 *ml.*)   1 *Tbs. sugar*
¼ *pt. wine or malt vinegar* (½ *c. or* 150 *ml.*)

Mix all together, stirring until the sugar is dissolved. Cover and leave to infuse for at least 2 hrs. before serving.

MUSHROOM SAUCE

Quantities for 4–8.

8 *oz. mushrooms* (250 *g.*)
1 *oz. butter* (25 *g.*) *or oil* (2 *Tbs.*)

Wash, drain, and slice or chop the mushrooms. Heat the butter or oil in a saucepan and stew the mushrooms until they begin to soften.

1 *oz. flour* (3 *Tbs. or* 25 *g.*)

Sprinkle this over the mushrooms and stir and cook for a few minutes longer.

½ *pt. stock* (1 *c. or* 250 *ml.*)   ¼ *pt. white wine* (½ *c. or* 150 *ml.*)

Add first the stock and then the wine, mixing well and stirring until the sauce boils. Boil for a few minutes.

Lemon juice   Salt and pepper

Season to taste and serve hot. If a smooth sauce is preferred, rub through a sieve or put in the electric blender. Re-heat if necessary and thin with more stock or wine as required.

MUSTARD SAUCE (Quick)

To serve with cooked fish or to use as a basting sauce for grills.

Quantities for 4.

2 *oz. butter* (50 *g.*)   4 *tsp. French mustard*

Melt these together and mix and stir well before using.

ONION SAUCE

Cooking Time 30 mins.   *Quantities* for 4.

> 8 *oz. onions* (250 *g.*)   1 *oz. butter or margarine* (25 *g.*)

Skin and slice the onions finely. Stew them in the melted fat until they are tender but not browned.

> 1 *Tbs. flour* $\frac{1}{2}$ *pt. milk* (1 *c.* or 250 *ml.*)
> *Salt and pepper*   *Ground nutmeg or mace*

Stir the flour into the onions and add the milk. Simmer for 15 mins. or until the onions are cooked. Serve as it is or, if a smooth sauce is preferred, either rub it through a sieve or mix smooth in the electric blender. Season to taste.

> *Cream (optional)*

Re-heat the sauce and thin with cream as desired.

PORTUGUESE MUSTARD SAUCE

Cooking Time about 10 mins.   *Quantities* for 4–6 or more, if used for a fondue.

> 2 *oz. butter* (50 *g.*)   2 *eggs*

Melt the butter in a small pan. Beat the eggs.

> 1 *Tbs. dry mustard*   1 *tsp. salt*   *Pinch of pepper*
> 2 *Tbs. sugar*   6 *Tbs. evaporated milk*

Mix the dry ingredients to a smooth cream with the vinegar and milk. Add to the melted butter, with the beaten eggs. Stir over a gentle heat or over boiling water until the mixture thickens. Serve hot or cold.

SALSA VERDE

Quantities for 8 or more.

> 4 *Tbs. olive oil* $\frac{1}{4}$ *pt. wine vinegar* ($\frac{1}{2}$ *c.* or 150 *ml.*)
> 2 *oz. roughly-cut parsley and stalks* (50 *g.*)
> 1 *oz. drained and rinsed capers* (25 *g.*)
> 1 *oz. pickled gherkins, or cucumber* (25 *g.*) *optional*
> *Pinch of dried garlic, or* $\frac{3}{4}$ *clove of fresh garlic*
> 1 *oz. bread* (1 *slice*), *or* 1 *small cooked potato*
> *Pepper, salt and a pinch of sugar*

Put all the ingredients in an electric blender and mix until smooth.

Alternative Method
Chop parsley, capers, gherkin and garlic. Crumb the bread, or sieve the potato. Beat all the ingredients together thoroughly.

SOUR CREAM SAUCE

This is very good with meat fondues and with hot or cold meats, fish and poultry.

Quantities for 4 or more.

> ½ *pt. sour or cultured cream* (1 *c. or* 250 *ml.*)
> ¼ *tsp. salt*   1 *Tbs. lemon juice*
> ¼ *tsp. freshly-ground white pepper*
> 1 *Tbs. chopped chives*

Combine ingredients thoroughly.

Alternative
For a less rich sauce use yogurt in place of the cream.

SOY SAUCE WITH GINGER

Quantities for 4.

> 4 *Tbs. soy sauce*   ½–1 *tsp. ground ginger*

Combine in a small saucepan, bring to the boil and use hot or cold.

TOMATO SAUCE, COLD

No. 1

Quantities for 4.

> 3 *Tbs. concentrated tomato purée*
> 2 *Tbs. soured or cultured cream*
> *Garlic salt to taste*   *Pepper*

Whisk together and chill before serving with meat or fish fondues or grills.

No. 2

Quantities for 4.

> 3 *Tbs. concentrated tomato purée*   3 *Tbs. plain yogurt*
> 1 *Tbs. lemon juice*   2 *Tbs. oil*
> ½ *tsp. salt*   ½ *tsp. sugar*
> *Pepper to taste*

Whisk together thoroughly.

3 *Tbs. chopped fresh herbs (tarragon, chives, parsley, marjoram)*
Mix into the sauce and chill before serving.

TOMATO SAUCE, HOT

Quantities for 4.

       ½ *pt. can condensed tomato soup (250 ml.)*
       1 *Tbs. tarragon vinegar*
       1 *tsp. brown sugar*
       1 *Tbs. Worcester sauce*   *Salt and pepper*

Mix all together, bring to the boil and serve.

VINAIGRETTE SAUCE

Quantities for 4.

    4 *Tbs. oil*   2 *Tbs. tarragon vinegar*
    1 *tsp. each of finely-chopped gherkin, shallot and parsley*
    Salt and pepper   ½ *tsp. made mustard.*

Mix together thoroughly.

YOGURT DRESSSING

Quantities for 4.

       1½ *Tbs. lemon juice*   *Pinch of pepper*
       ¼ *tsp. made mustard*   ¼ *tsp. salt*

Mix together in a small bowl.

       ¼ *pt. yogurt (½ c. or 150 ml.)*

Stir into the other mixture until well blended, and chill for ½ hr. before serving.

18 Salads and other Accompaniments

Included here are recipes for salads suitable for serving in place of hot vegetables with fondues, grills and other dishes. I have not included ordinary vegetable cookery, but there are some recipes for grilled vegetables, potatoes cooked in the electric frypan, and for rice as an accompaniment.

BRUSSELS SPROUTS AND CELERY SALAD

Quantities. Allow about 2–3 sprouts and a small stick of celery per person.

> *Firm, raw brussels sprouts   Crisp sticks of raw celery*
> *mayonnaise, page 168, or French dressing, page 176, or*
> *yogurt dressing, page 181*
> *Hard-boiled eggs or coloured vegetables to garnish*

Wash the vegetables and drain thoroughly. Slice thinly and mix in equal quantities. Combine at once with the salad dressing and garnish to taste.

BRUSSELS SPROUTS AND ORANGE SALAD

Quantities for 4.

> 8 *oz. brussels sprouts* (250 g.)   2 *large oranges*

Wash and drain the sprouts and slice them as finely as possible. Peel the oranges, remove all pith and divide them in segments. Mix sprouts and oranges together, reserving a few orange segments to garnish the top of the salad.

> *Mayonnaise, page 168, or yogurt dressing, page 181*

Combine the salad with enough dressing to moisten, and garnish with orange segments.

This salad goes particularly well with pork fondue or kebabs, or with other pork dishes.

CABBAGE, CELERY AND APPLE SALAD

Quantities for 4.

> 2 *sticks celery, chopped*   1 *carrot, grated*
> 6 *oz. very finely shredded raw cabbage heart* (2 *c. or* 175 *g.*)
> 1 *dessert apple, peeled, cored and chopped*
> *Salad dressing to moisten*

Mix all ingredients together and garnish to taste.

Alternative

Substitute shredded brussels sprouts for the cabbage. Use curry mayonnaise, page 169, for the salad dressing.

CARROT AND APPLE SALAD

This can be made in advance, as the lemon dressing prevents the apples from turning brown. It makes an unusual and delicious carrot salad.

Quantities for 4.

> 8 *oz. carrots* (250 *g.*)

Wash, scrape and grate the carrots moderately finely. Put them in a bowl.

> 4 *Tbs. lemon juice*   2 *oz. sugar* (4 *Tbs. or* 50 *g.*)
> *Finely-grated rind of* 1 *lemon*

Mix together until the sugar dissolves and pour over the carrots.

> 2 *small apples*

Peel, core and grate. Mix with the carrots and serve.

CHICORY SALAD

Quantities Allow ½ lb. chicory (250 g.) for 2–3 people.

Wash and drain the chicory and slice it across thinly. Dress with French dressing, page 176, or yogurt dressing, page 181, and serve alone or combined with other salad vegetables.

CHICORY AND OLIVE SALAD

Quantities for 4.

> 4–8 *pieces of chicory*   8 *stoned and chopped green olives*
> *French dressing, page* 181;   *Chopped tarragon*

Slice the chicory finely or chop it. Mix with the olives and dressing and serve sprinkled with the tarragon.

CHICORY AND ORANGE SALAD

This uses just the rind—leaving the whole oranges for a fruit salad or other dish.

Quantities for 4.

> 8 *small or 4 large pieces of chicory*

Wash and drain.

> 2 *oranges*

Scrub the skins and then peel the orange part off thinly. Cut this in very thin, fine strips and boil them in plenty of water for 5–6 mins. Drain and allow to become cold.

> ½ *Tbs. French mustard*
> ¼ *pt. double cream or cultured cream (½ c. or 150 ml.)*
> *Salt and pepper   Cayenne pepper*

Mix the mustard and cream and season the dressing well. Cut the pieces of chicory in half lengthwise and remove the hard core at the base. Cut the leaves in pieces of a suitable size to eat with a fork. Put them in a serving dish, sprinkle with the orange rind and serve the dressing separately.

GRAPEFRUIT AND BEETROOT SALAD

Quantities for 4.

> 2 *large grapefruit*

Peel, and remove all pith. Divide into segments or slice into circles, removing pips.

> 2 *medium-sized cooked beetroot*

Skin and slice.

> 1 *lettuce*

Wash and dry, and use the leaves to line a salad bowl or flat dish. Arrange on it alternately the grapefruit and beetroot.

> *French dressing, page* 181

Pour it over the beetroot and fruit just before serving.

MIXED GREEN SALAD

Most green vegetables are suitable. Choose from the following, according to season:

Wash and dry carefully, and combine at the last minute with French dressing, page 181.

To make the vegetables fresh and crisp wash in advance, drain well and put in a covered dish in the refrigerator for several hours or overnight. Then shred or otherwise prepare them for the salad.

MUSHROOM SALAD, RAW

Raw button mushrooms
French dressing, page 181, made with lemon juice instead of vinegar
Chopped parsley   Finely-chopped garlic (optional)

Wash and drain the mushrooms. Slice them very thinly and dress with plenty of French dressing and chopped parsley. Use a little garlic if liked.

MUSHROOM SALAD, COOKED

Cooking Time 5 mins.   *Quantities* for 4.

8 oz. mushrooms (250 g.)

Wash and drain and boil them in a very little salted water until they are just tender. Drain and cool, then slice thinly.

2 thin slices of raw onion	*2 tsp. sugar*
2 Tbs. thick cream	*Freshly-ground pepper*
Salt	*1–2 Tbs. lemon juice*

Chop the onion very finely and mix it with the other ingredients, seasoning to taste. Add the mushrooms and combine gently. Serve in a salad bowl, and sprinkle the top of the salad with

Chopped parsley

ORANGE SALAD

Quantities for 4.

4 oranges

Peel the oranges and remove all pith. Slice into thin rounds removing the pips.

Chopped fresh tarragon and chervil

Sprinkle over the oranges.

186

2 *Tbs olive oil*   1 *Tbs. vinegar*   2 *tsp. lemon juice*

Mix these, and pour them over the oranges. Leave to stand for a while.

Watercress

Serve the salad on individual plates and garnish with watercress.

ORANGE AND ONION SALAD

Quantities for 4.

4 *medium oranges*

Peel them and slice very thinly over a plate to catch all the juice. Remove pips, and put the fruit in a shallow dish, reserving the juice.

1 *small onion, finely-chopped*   4 *Tbs. olive oil*   ½ *tsp. salt*

Combine with the orange juice. Pour over the oranges, and leave to marinate for 20 mins.

Lettuce leaves

Arrange the orange slices on a bed of lettuce leaves.

SWEET PEPPER SALAD

Use green or red sweet peppers.

Raw

Wash well, cut in half and remove seeds and white pith. Slice very thinly and dress with French dressing, page 181, or mix with other salad vegetables.

Cooked

Wash, cut in half and remove seeds and white pith. Grill them skin side up until the skin can easily be peeled off (a few mins.). Then slice and dress as before.

TOMATO AND SWEET PEPPER SALAD

Canned red peppers   *Ripe tomatoes*
French dressing, page 181

Drain the peppers thoroughly and slice them. Wash and slice the tomatoes. Combine them in equal amounts, and pour the French dressing over them.

Finely-chopped onion (*optional*)

Sprinkle on top.

GRILLED APPLES AND CHEESE

To serve as a snack on their own, or as an accompaniment to grilled or fried meat.

Cooking Time a few mins.   *Quantities* for 4.

*4 medium-sized dessert apples   4 Tbs. grated cheese
Oil or melted butter*

Peel the apples and remove centres with an apple corer. Cut each across to make four thick rings. Put in the grill pan or on a rack, brush the top sides with melted butter or oil. Sprinkle on the cheese, and grill until the cheese melts and browns.

GRILLED AUBERGINES

Method 1

Cooking Time 15–20 mins. *Quantities* for 4.

2–4 aubergines   Salt and pepper   Olive oil

Wash and dry the aubergines. Remove the stem end. Cut them in half lengthwise, and put them in a single layer cut side up, in a shallow dish. Sprinkle with salt and pepper and brush with olive oil to coat them well. Leave to marinate for 1 hr. or more.

Grill them under a moderate heat until they are tender and browned on top. When they are beginning to brown, brush with more oil.

Serve as a garnish for fried or grilled meat.

Method 2

Peel the aubergines and cut them in $\frac{1}{2}$ in. (1 cm.) slices. Mix oil and seasonings in the proportion of 1 Tbs. oil with $\frac{1}{4}$ tsp. salt and a pinch of pepper. Dip the slices of aubergine in this and grill them 3 mins. on each side or until tender. Serve plain, or with grated cheese sprinkled on top.

GRILLED BANANAS

To serve with grilled bacon rashers or gammon, or as a garnish for pork or chicken, roast, grilled or fried.

Cooking Time about 8 mins.   *Quantities* 1 banana per person.

Peel the bananas, brush with melted butter or margarine and grill under a moderate heat until they are tender, turning once.

GRILLED MUSHROOMS

Use medium to large mushrooms. Remove the stalks and wash the mushrooms; drain, gills down. Grill them gill sides up with a knob of butter in each one. Grill gently until just tender. A few minutes is all that they require.

GRILLED SWEET PEPPERS

Wash the peppers, cut them in half lengthwise, remove seeds and white pith. Leave in halves or cut in smaller pieces according to taste. Brush with oil and grill until just tender, turning once during cooking.

GRILLED TOMATOES

Wash the tomatoes, cut them in halves, season and grill, cut side up, under a moderate heat until they are tender, about 10 mins. If liked, brush with oil or put a small knob of butter on each cut surface before grilling.

GRILLED POTATO AND CHEESE BALLS

These are for serving with any meat or fish dish. If they are to go with grilled meat or fish, grill them at the same time, or cook first and keep hot.

Cooking Time ¾ hr.—which includes time for boiling the potatoes. *Quantities* for 4.

1 *lb. potatoes* (½ *kg.*)

Boil in their jackets, skin and mash, or put through a ricer.

½ *oz. butter or margarine* (15 g.)   3 *oz. grated cheese* (75 g.)
Salt and pepper   *Pinch of ground mace*   *Chopped parsley*

Beat into the hot potatoes and leave until cool enough to handle. Roll into balls and grill until brown all over. If preferred, they can be made into small flat cakes and will then only require one turning during grilling. If made in advance and allowed to become cold they will need 15–20 mins.' grilling to heat through and brown.

PARISIAN POTATOES

For the frypan.

Cooking Time 10–15 mins.   *Quantities* for 4.

1–1½ *lb. potatoes* (½–¾ *kg.*)

Peel the potatoes and cut them in small cubes.

Heat the frypan at 380° (190°C) and when it is up to temperature add just enough butter or oil to make a thin film on the surface. Fry the potatoes, turning frequently, until they are well browned and cooked through.

Chopped parsley or chives   Salt and pepper

Sprinkle the herbs over the potatoes, season to taste, and serve.

SAUTÉ POTATOES

The frypan gives a crisp brown result with the minimum amount of fat or oil, and has the advantage of a large surface to take plenty of potatoes.

Cut the cold boiled potatoes into slices $\frac{1}{4}$–$\frac{1}{2}$ in. thick ($\frac{1}{2}$–1 cm.).

Heat the frypan to 400° (200°C), and when it is up to temperature add a little oil or fat and tilt the pan to give an even coating to the surface. Add the potatoes and brown on both sides.

Serve, sprinkled with salt and pepper and chopped parsley, or mixed green herbs.

SAUTÉ POTATOES WITH CHEESE

This makes a good, quick snack. Serve it with a green salad or with fresh fruit to follow.

Sauté cooked potatoes as in the previous recipe and when they are browned sprinkle them liberally with well-flavoured grated cheese. Cook until the cheese begins to melt and then serve.

Variation
Fry a little finely-chopped onion with the potatoes.

RICE WITH HERBS

Cooking Time about 15 mins.   *Quantities* for 4.

8 oz. *long-grain rice (1 c. or 250 g.)*
1 *pt. cold water (2 c. or $\frac{1}{2}$ l.)*   1 *tsp. salt*

Wash the rice by putting it in a sieve and running cold water through it. Put in a pan with the water and salt. Bring to the boil, stir once and cover. Simmer for 15 mins. without lifting the lid. Test a few grains to see if it is cooked. Fluff it up with a fork, cover and put in a warm place for a few mins.

Chopped fresh herbs (*thyme, parsley, chives, marjoram*)

Add plenty of the herbs to give a good flavour, using just one herb, or a mixture according to the dish it will accompany.

FRIED RICE

Left-over cold boiled rice can be used for this. Fry a little finely-chopped onion in butter or oil until it is soft and beginning to brown. Add dry cooked rice and stir and heat until all the fat is absorbed and the rice is beginning to brown.

Optional additions
   Chopped canned pineapple and chopped salted almonds.
   Raisins and chopped almonds.
   Chopped green peppers fried with the onion.
   Ground spices to taste.

RISOTTO

For frypan or hotplate.

Cooking Time 25–30 mins.   *Quantities* for 4–6.

2 oz. fat or oil (4 *Tbs.*)   6 *oz. onions* (175 *g.*)

Skin and chop the onions. Heat the frypan at about 320° (160°C), and when it is up to temperature add the fat or oil. Fry the onions until they are just beginning to brown.

12 *oz. long-grain rice* (1½ *c. or* 375 *g.*)

Add to the pan, and cook for a few minutes, stirring all the time with a wooden spoon.

2 *pt. stock* (1 *l.*) *or use chicken cubes and water*

Add to the rice and stir until it boils. Turn the heat down to about 300° (150°C) to keep it bubbling gently in the uncovered pan. Stir gently from time to time. By the time the rice is cooked, all the liquid should be absorbed. Turn the heat down to keep it hot, but not enough to continue cooking.

Flavouring additions can be any of the following:
   Plenty of chopped cooked herbs; chopped sweet peppers; chopped tomatoes; sliced cooked mushrooms or drained, canned mushrooms; diced cooked liver or kidney; diced left-over meat. Salt and pepper.
Add these, and allow to become hot before serving.

Grated Parmesan cheese

Hand separately to be sprinkled on when the risotto is served.

SAFFRON RICE

Cooking Time 20–25 mins.   *Quantities* for 4.

8 *oz. long-grain rice* (1 *c. or* 250 *g.*)
1 *pt. stock or water* (2 *c. or* ½ *l.*)   1 *tsp. salt*   2 *bay leaves*
A good pinch each of ground cloves and cinnamon
Pepper   Saffron

Saffron is sold either powdered or in dried shreds. The shreds can be powdered in a mortar, or else used to make an infusion by pouring a little boiling water over them and leaving them to soak until cold. Then strain and put any surplus liquid in a bottle for future use. Powdered saffron is sprinkled dry into the rice, whereas the liquid can be added to the cooking water to make it yellow.

Put all the ingredients in a pan, bring to the boil, stir and cover. Reduce the heat to simmering temperature, or put the pan in a moderate oven. Test the rice after 15 mins. to see if it is cooked through (no hard core in the middle when squeezed in the fingers). All the water should be absorbed by this time. To dry it, fluff with a fork, cover, and stand it in a warm place for 5–10 mins. Do not leave it hot enough to go on cooking, or it will become a sticky mass. Remove the bay leaves before serving. It will keep in good condition for some time if put on a warming plate on the side table.

19 Glossary of Terms

ALMONDS, toasted or roasted

These are blanched or skinned almonds which have been fried brown
in a little oil or butter, or baked in a moderate oven with a little
butter. Drain on absorbent paper.

BLENDER, or Liquidiser

A machine for blending ingredients at very high speed, either to produce a liquid or to make a pulp or purée, depending on the amount of
liquid either in the food or added to it.

BLENDING

Is the thorough mixing of ingredients to give a smooth texture or an
even consistency. It can be used to describe mixing dry ingredients
with a liquid to give a smooth paste, or for mixing two dry or two wet
ingredients together.

BORDER MOULD

This is a circular mould with a hole in the middle, also called a ring
mould. It is used for cooking some savoury dishes, but more often
for yeast and cake mixtures. It is also used for moulding rice to
serve with curries and other dishes served with rice. The cooked food
is put in the centre of the unmoulded rice.

BUTTERED CRUMBS, see page 160. (Crab Scallops)

CANDLE WARMERS

These are food warmers heated by means of candles, special short,
wide ones, sold for the purpose. Some warmers are single burners,

others have a pair of candles. They are only warmers, and will not give sufficient heat for cooking.

CHARCOAL

Is considered to be the best material for making a fire for grilling. It needs good ventilation, otherwise the fumes can be dangerous. It is safest when used out of doors. Pieces of charcoal for cooking purposes are sold in bags. When using charcoal grills follow the instructions provided by the manufacturer.

CHAUFFE SAUCE or SAUCE WARMER (Fig. 9)

This is usually a small metal or ceramic saucepan with a long handle. The pan is supported on a tripod over a gentle heat, usually a candle heater. It is invaluable for serving sauces, especially melted butter. I also use mine for warming spirit for a flambé, see pages 51–3.

CHOPS

These may be lamb, mutton, veal or pork and consist of loin chops taken from the lower part of the spine where the bones are short. They have shorter bones and more meat than cutlets, see below. Chump chops come from the end of the spine and have a bone in the middle.

CLARIFIED BUTTER

Used for frying when a butter that won't brown is required. Butter is melted in a small pan, the scum removed with a spoon and the sediment allowed to settle in the bottom of the pan. The clear butter is then carefully poured off. This is the clarified butter. The scum and sediment can be used for dressing cooked vegetables.

COATING—or, To coat

To cover one food with a thin layer of another in liquid form. Usually applied to food dipped in beaten egg or in a batter.

CREAM

Creams are classified according to their fat content. Single cream has 18 per cent fat, double cream 48 per cent, canned cream 23 per cent. Both single and double cream are used in cooking. When the cream

194

9. Chauffe sauce (sauce warmer) for heating brandy and liqueurs.
White metal top and candle holder, black iron support.

has to be boiled to make a sauce, double must be used as the single is liable to curdle and will not thicken the sauce properly.

For whipping, double cream is used, or a mixture of half double and half single.

Cultured cream or sour cream is cream inoculated with micro-organisms to produce souring and thickening. It can be used in place of single or double cream in cooking, and it adds a sharp flavour to the product.

CUTLET

This may be lamb, mutton, veal or pork, and it comes from the upper part of the spine where there are long rib bones. There is only a small amount of meat, called the 'eye', but it is usually tender and succulent.

DICING

Dice are small cubes obtained by cutting the food into strips and the strips across into small bits.

DOUBLE BOILER

This is a double saucepan. The top part holds the food and the lower part has water. For cooking, the water is kept boiling rapidly and the food cooks by steam. This is particularly useful for foods which are inclined to over-cook or stick to the pan when put on a direct heat, especially if it is a naked flame. For keeping food warm, the water is kept hot, not boiling. When using a double boiler, cooking can be hastened by putting the upper part of the boiler over a direct heat until the food is hot, and then putting it over the boiling water to finish cooking.

EGG GRADES

Large eggs are not less than $2\frac{3}{16}$ oz. in weight.

Standard eggs are not less than $1\frac{7}{8}$ oz., and this is the size used in all recipes unless otherwise stated. The weight is usually taken as 2 oz. or 56 g.

Medium eggs are not less than $1\frac{5}{8}$ oz.

Small eggs are not less than $1\frac{1}{2}$ oz. Thus, 4 small eggs can be used instead of 2 standard eggs.

ESCALOPE

A thin piece of boneless meat weighing 2–3 oz. (see veal escalope).

'EYE' OF A CUTLET

The meaty portion. It can be removed from the bone and used to make an escalope by beating it out thinly with a cutlet bat or wooden rolling pin.

FILLET STEAK

Is the most tender beef steak, and comes from the sirloin ribs. It is the smaller of the two pieces of meat on a sirloin and is sometimes called 'undercut' or 'tenderloin'. It is often removed from the carcase in one long piece and sold like that, or sliced into portions.

FISH FILLET

A piece of a whole fish removed from the bone. Large fillets are sold cut in portions. A round fish yields two fillets, a flat fish four.

FISH STEAKS

Pieces of fish cut across the body with the spine bone in the middle.
Steaks from the tail end of the fish have the best shape.

FOOD WARMERS, see page 10.

FORCEMEAT is another name for stuffing.

FRENCH BREAD

This usually means the thin, open-textured loaves with a lot of crisp
crust. Very thin loaves are known as French sticks.

GINGER, fresh

This is the fresh rhizome of the ginger plant. The rhizome is also used in
various preserved forms: dried and ground; dried in pieces for flavouring pickles; and preserved in syrup. Fresh ginger is the type used in a
Chinese hotpot (see page 45), and is sold by many Chinese and
Indian shops.

GIRDLE or GRIDDLE

The old girdle was a very heavy, cast-iron circular plate with a handle
over the top. It was either hung over an open fire, or put on top of a
stove. Some modern electric and gas cookers provide a girdle for
using on the hotplate or burner. These are designed for cooking the
traditional girdle scones and cakes, and also for cooking eggs and
meat. Portable automatic electric girdles are available, and the
electric frypan can be used as a girdle, see pages 128 and 158.

HEAT-RESISTANT DISHES

These are dishes which can stand baking temperatures. They may be
made of specially-treated ceramic or glass, enamelled steel, enamelled
cast-iron, copper, stainless-steel or aluminium alloy. The metal ones
can usually be safely put on the hotplate or burner as well as used in
the oven.

METAL SERVING DISHES

These are the best for flambés, as they are unaffected by the high temperatures generated. Stainless-steel, silver-plated or aluminium alloy are the most commonly used, though enamelled cast-iron is suitable for some flambés.

MUSTARD

The kinds used in cooking are referred to as 'dry' mustard—meaning the powder out of a tin. 'Prepared' mustard means dry mustard mixed to a paste with water or milk (English mustard); and French mustard the kind which is sold ready mixed with oil, vinegar and flavourings.

OMELET PANS

These are little pans with curved sides and a base about 6–7 in. across (15–18 cm.). Many people never make an omelet in anything else. I find a general-purpose, good-quality aluminium frying pan is perfectly adequate, provided that the inside is kept smooth by cleaning with steel wool soap pads and then dried thoroughly before use.

PEPPER

Those used in cooking include black and white peppers, which may be purchased as peppercorns and ground in a pepper mill. White pepper is sold ready-ground. Cayenne (Chilli) pepper is very hot and is used in tiny amounts. Paprika pepper is a mild red pepper with the flavour of sweet peppers or pimientos. Jamaica pepper is a spice, allspice, like large black peppercorns. It is also sold ground.

POACHING

Cooking foods such as eggs or fish in water, or other liquid, just to cover. The liquid is kept below boiling point, and the food—which is cooked very gently—remains tender and keeps its shape.

PORK FILLET

The meat from loin chops removed in one piece, long and narrow and weighing from $\frac{1}{2}$–$\frac{3}{4}$ lb. (250–375 g.). It is usually sold in the piece. Pork fillet may also be a boneless slice from the top of the leg.

POTATO FLOUR

A flour made from the starch extracted from potatoes, usually sold in packets and often labelled 'fécule de pomme de terre'. It has certain advantages over ordinary flour or cornflour when it is used for thickening liquids. It is cooked as soon as the liquid boils, and it gives a very clear, shiny sauce, specially useful with fruit sauces.

POUSSIN

A frying or grilling chicken, also called a 'broiler'.

RÔTISSERIE

A spit-roaster for cooking joints of meat or kebabs (see pages 143–4).

ROUX

A mixture of fat and flour used for thickening sauces. The fat is melted, the flour stirred in and cooked for a few mins. for a white roux, longer for a brown roux. After that the liquid is added, and the flavourings and the sauce cooked some more.

SAFFRON

This is made from the dried stigmas of the saffron crocus (see page 192).

SAUTÉ

Comes from the French 'sauter' meaning 'to jump', and is shallow frying carried out in a pan deeper than the usual frying pan and with a lid (see pages 111).

SEASONED FLOUR

1 *Tbs. salt*   4 *oz. flour* ($\frac{3}{4}$ *c. or* 125 *g.*) $\frac{1}{2}$ *tsp. pepper*

Sift these together and keep the flour in a dredger for dusting meat and fish before cooking.

SIMMERING

Cooking below boiling point, about 183° (85°C). The surface of the liquid is agitated, but not bubbling.

SLIVERS

Very fine strips, like splinters, usually of vegetables.

SPINACH, leaf

Spinach cooked and served without sieving.

SPIRIT BURNERS

Small heaters which use methylated spirits for fuel. Some burn the solid counterpart of methylated spirits, methaldehyde, which is used in picnic stoves.

SPIT-ROASTING, see page 143.

TRIVET

A three-legged metal stand for holding a cooking pot. Variations of the trivet are used for fondue and flambé sets (see page 14).

VEAL ESCALOPES

These are very thin slices of veal and should be cut from the fillet —which is either the top part of the leg or rump, or else the under-part of the loin or backbone. The slices are beaten to make them very thin. The butcher will usually do this for you.

Index

202